Praise for Love, Unstuck & Christy Holt

Reading *Love, Unstuck* is like having a heart-to-heart with a friend who gets it. But Christy is so much more. She is an experienced coach with unique methods, practical tools, and a fresh approach to transforming first yourself, then your relationships. So if you identify as a people pleaser or have problems with setting and enforcing boundaries then, you need Christy. If you are sick of being tired of being in crappy relationships, then run—don't walk—to BUY THIS BOOK!

-**Akosua Brown**, Miracle Mindset Mentor & Creativity Coach, Best-Selling Author, and Recovering People Pleaser

Christy Holt has written a complete and comprehensive relationship guidebook—the ultimate relationship book, filled with tools, insight, and case studies. Christy's playful but informed writing style sets this book apart from others in its genre and keeps the reader inspired and interested. This is a must-read for anyone looking to improve their feelings about themselves and the important relationships in their lives.

-**Kelly Bramblett**, Best-Selling Author of the *Shadow Work Journal and Guide for Beginners*

Everyone on the planet should be reading this. Engaging. Requires the reader to take a deep look into themselves and the "why" of their behavior and hopefully recognize where and how they can make some positive internal changes.

-**Jeanette Sherman**, Best-Selling Author

Christy Holt's voice cuts through the noise with refreshing clarity and irresistible spice! Her unwavering authenticity sets her apart in the personal growth space—there's zero fluff, just powerful truth-telling that transforms lives. This book is your roadmap to wholeness, teaching what so many miss: that the journey to extraordinary love begins with you. A must-read for anyone seeking to level up their love life from a thought leader who embodies what she teaches. Holt's approach is revolutionary yet real, showing you how to build the foundation you need before choosing the partnership you deserve.

-Elvira V. Hopper, Founder of the Miracle Magnet Movement

This brilliant book flows seamlessly from personal growth to practical relationship guidance, striking the perfect balance between accessibility and depth. As a relationship expert writing with warmth and wisdom, the author presents scientifically-grounded insights in a refreshingly approachable way. The bite-sized chapters and simple yet powerful exercises make transformation feel achievable rather than overwhelming.

What stands out is the book's profound yet digestible message that relationships are opportunities to give, grow, and learn with intention. It's an invaluable resource whether you're healing from past relationships, seeking new love, or wanting to strengthen your current partnership.

This is essential reading for anyone feeling stuck in their relationship journey—offering professional-level insights in an accessible format that empowers readers to begin their transformation, with or without additional coaching. The author's engaging style makes complex relationship concepts not just understandable, but actionable. A must-read that will undoubtedly change lives!

-Lindsey Troumbly, Holistic Life Coach

This book is heartfelt, empowering, and filled with useful tools. An incredibly helpful and top-notch resource for anyone looking to improve their relationships and find self-love.

-**Stephen Komolafe**, Writer, Editor, and Illustrator

This might be the book I didn't know I needed. Christy's journey from feeling invisible and unfulfilled in relationships to discovering the power of self-love and inner growth is truly inspiring. By sharing her struggles, she shows how true fulfillment starts from within. This book helps you break free from bad habits and build better relationships.

-**Frankie Cameron**, Best-Selling Author of *Hollow Edge*

Also by the Author

Unstuck (for women): Break Free from Self-Doubt and Stop Over-thinking Using the Spiral Stopper Method to Take Control of Your Emotions, Build Confidence & Self Love

Unstuck for Women Daily Self Discovery Journal: 90 Days of Gratitude and Self Discovery Prompts to Build Confidence & Self Love

Sweary AF Colouring Meditations: Release Your Inner Unicorn with Bold Lines & Badass Mantras

Abundant AF Colouring Meditations: Watch Your Prosperity Potential Blossom with Abundance Affirmations & Money Mantras

Run For Your Life: Lessons Learned from Going the Distance

Love, unstuck

Creating Healthy, Happy Relationships through Self-Love, Emotional Intelligence, and Authentic Connection

CHRISTY HOLT

Dedication

*This book is dedicated to the most incredible human who unconditionally loves and accepts me just as I am, every single day. You are my favorite across all categories and I f*cking love you infinitely.*

Welcome, Gorgeous Human!

HAVE YOU EVER FELT like you're constantly giving your all in relationships, only to end up feeling unseen, unheard, and unfulfilled?

You're not alone.

I've been there, too—slumped on the bathroom floor, bawling, nearly drowning in a puddle of my own tears while I questioned my worth and wondered why my relationships kept leaving me feeling empty and exhausted. I had tried all the things—reading self-help books, going to therapy, attempting to communicate better—but **something was still missing**.

As I exited my second marriage, I told myself, *Never again! Relationships are far more hassle than they are worth*. I just wasn't interested in having to contort myself to make another one work. So, as I donned the title of divorcée for the second time, I decided to refocus my sights on something I *could* control: creating a life for myself that I truly loved.

As I turned inward, I realized that in my previous relationships I had tried so fucking hard to be "lovable" that I was struggling to recognize the "me" that I had become. The happy-go-lucky me had been replaced by an anxious, desperate, and unhappy shell of myself.

And that's when I realized the truth—I didn't have a relationship problem, I had an identity problem.

I had been looking for love in all the wrong places. I was seeking fulfillment and validation from others, instead of cultivating it within myself. I knew that I had a lot of love to give, and that I wanted to give it freely. But I deserved to receive some love back too, didn't I? What I had been doing wasn't working, and I knew that if I wanted a different result, *I had to do something differently*. This realization led me on a messy, yet oh-so-fucking-beautiful adventure of self-discovery and transformation. And now, I'm inviting you to link arms and set off on this journey to get unstuck and create the conscious, fulfilling relationships you deserve.

By picking up this book, you've already taken a brave step towards reclaiming your power and redefining what love means to you. Whether you're single, dating, or in a long-term partnership, the principles and tools in these pages will guide you to break free from patterns that no longer serve you and create a love story that lights you TF up from the inside out.

In my previous book, *Unstuck for Women*, I described how you can ditch self-doubt, navigate overthinking and overwhelm, and cultivate confidence and self-love. Now, in *Love, Unstuck*, we'll take it one step further. We will explore the myths and mindsets that keep us trapped in unfulfilling relationships. You'll learn how to cultivate unshakable self-love, communicate your needs and boundaries with confidence, and navigate life's challenges with grace and resilience. Only when you can do this—respect and love yourself—will you be able to call in a love that does this too.

Through practical exercises, real-life examples, and heartfelt stories, you'll gain the tools to create the passionate, purposeful relationships you've always craved. These tools have been transformative not only in my own life but in the lives of countless others I've had the privilege of adventuring alongside of. And while this book contains everything you need to begin your journey, I'm also here to support you through additional resources, including courses and mentorship, whenever you're ready to dive deeper. So, my dear friend, are you ready to get unstuck and discover a love that makes you feel completely fucking alive? Let's dive in together, with open hearts and curious minds.

Your messy, beautiful adventure awaits.

♡ *Christy*

(AKA The Happiness Hussy)

A Note on Perspective: While the insights and tools in this book come primarily from my experience as a cisgender, heterosexual, white woman, the core principles of self-discovery, authentic connection, and conscious relationship building are universal. Regardless of where you land on the spectrum of human experience, this book is meant to serve as a guide for your unique journey. **Your path to love may look different from mine, and that's not just 'okay'—it's beautiful!** What matters most is the relationship you build with yourself, as that forms the foundation for all other connections in your life.

The exercises and principles in this book are adaptable to your individual circumstances, beliefs, and relationship structures. I invite you to *try things on*, then take what resonates and leave what doesn't, knowing that *you* are the ultimate expert on your own experience.

Table of Contents

Part 3 Creating Conscious Relationships

Who This Book is For

THIS BOOK IS FOR the whole-ass humans out there seeking a love that makes them truly happy. If you've been on a rollercoaster of unfulfilling relationships, self-help books, couples therapy sessions, and failed attempts at communication, this book is your invitation to get off that wild ride and chart a new path.

When it comes to our human existence, relationships are foundational. Every aspect of our lives is intertwined with relationships, whether with family, friends, colleagues, romantic partners, ourselves, or perfect strangers. It can feel incredibly challenging to find meaningful relationships in a world that pits us against one another and encourages the constant struggle to "be better." Despite how "connected" we are today, loneliness is on the rise and related mental health challenges are more prevalent than ever. We are, of course, each on our own journeys, yet **we're not meant to navigate life's complexities alone**. These connections serve as the cornerstone of our existence, providing us with companionship, support, and a sense of belonging and fulfillment.

Our interactions with others shape our perspectives, challenge our assumptions, and help us grow as individuals. They offer us comfort in times of distress, laughter in moments of joy, and a shoulder to lean on when we need it most. Through our interactions with others, we gain valuable insights about our strengths, weaknesses, and values. It is within relationships that we learn to navigate complex emotions, communicate effectively, and cultivate empathy and understanding.

Moreover, **our relationships serve as mirrors**, reflecting aspects of ourselves that we may not be aware of. They provide us with opportunities for self-reflection, growth, and transformation. Relationships also play a crucial role when it comes to self-discovery and personal development.

In addition to interpersonal relationships, we also have important relationships with our body (AKA our meatsuit), our external experiences with the world, our existing belief systems, and even with other inanimate objects (i.e. food or money). What we are going to cover in this book has the potential to impact it all!

Ultimately, relationships are at the heart of what it means to be human. They enrich our lives, give us purpose, and provide us with the love and connection we need to thrive. As you are reading, you may be realizing that you rarely share your thoughts and feelings—because you never feel seen or heard with your partner anyway. Deep down you know you deserve a fulfilling love life and relationships that spark joy and excitement, but you feel stuck because *you've been waiting* to find "the one" or for your partner to reignite the spark you need. If your desire is to experience unconditional love, deeper connections, and fulfillment in your relationships (and I know you do), read on!

This book is for YOU if:

- You wish to repair or improve a difficult relationship

- You are ready to reignite the passion in your relationship

- You can't help but wonder if this is *all there is* when it comes to experiencing love and connection

- You long to experience true intimacy and create a deep, meaningful connection with another

- You desire to feel truly seen, heard, loved and accepted

With the tools in this book, you can:

- Interrupt the patterns and habits that keep you *stuck* in the familiar

- Find freedom from people pleasing and perfection-chasing

- Stop "walking on eggshells" to avoid yet another fight

- Build emotional intelligence and cultivate a safe environment for sharing your thoughts and feelings

- Improve your communication skills, boundaries, and ability to clearly ask for what you desire

- Build a greater understanding of yourself and what makes you incredible

When you're ready to rediscover the passion in your love life, you will reap the benefits of improving your communication skills, boundaries, and ability to clearly ask for what you desire. If you've stopped asking for what you really want, it's probably because you think it won't matter anyway—your reality may seem so far from the dream that the chasm seems impossible to cross. But through this book, you'll rediscover and get what most of us want:

- Better intimacy and deeper connection

- Improved emotional intelligence

- A greater understanding of yourself

Imagine how free it feels to live a life with no masks, no chasing perfection, no waiting on anyone else, and no struggling or hustling to keep everyone else around you happy. **You get to both be yourself AND replace your anxiety with peace and joy.** Talk about a win-win! If your desire is to live life YOUR way, then this book is definitely for you. I'm so freaking excited at what lies ahead for you!

Now that you know what's possible, I'm going to share why this journey is so personal to me, and how my own path through relationship struggles led to the insights and tools you'll find in these coming pages.

Why I Wrote This Book

LIFE IS TOO SHORT for relationships that don't light you up. *Forget mediocre. No more settling.* **You deserve a "fuck yes" relationship!**

Before we dive in, I want you to know that everything in this book comes from lived experience, not just theoretical knowledge. My insights are forged from personal transformation, countless conversations, and real-world trial and error. Well aware that I don't have all the "right answers," I'm passionate about learning and exploring diverse perspectives to uncover common themes.

What makes this book different? **I believe that YOU already have your own answers**. My role isn't to tell you what to do—it's to help you remember what you already know. Consider this book an invitation to try on some different perspectives and see what resonates with you.

I believe that incredible relationships are available for everyone who wants one. As much as you point your finger and think that "they" are the reason for your unhappiness, it's actually you. And since it's you, if you want an incredible relationship, you can make it happen and you 100% deserve it.

Everything changed for me when I realized that the key to experiencing the love I desired was within me.

I learned that by taking **radical responsibility for your own experience**, you create an opportunity for real impact (and creating the legacy you dream about). Why? Because you're focused on the one thing you *can* control: **yourself**. It can feel safer to shift responsibility away from yourself through blaming, justifying, or complaining, but when you do this, you give away your power and keep yourself trapped in struggle patterns.

I wish I could say that I learned everything I needed to know out of the first one *or two or three* relationships, but the learning was unfortunately more of a slow drip for me. By the time my second divorce was underway, it became clear that this would not merely be the end of another relationship for me. This life-altering change in relationship status had me taking a complete inventory of what was and wasn't working in my life. Eventually concluding that I could not / would not repeat these patterns even one more time, I knew I had to do things differently moving forward.

My first step was to do some *unlearning* and get myself out of survival mode—the incredible tools for which I will be sharing in Parts 1 and 2 of this book. My approach is somewhat different to others in this space, and I cannot wait to show you how some small perspective shifts may alter your experience of relationships in the most wonderful way.

Only once I held a new perspective could I begin to get unstuck (Part 2). Once unstuck, I was able to start building the skills needed to create the life and love I really wanted. Because *true life wisdom is best shared with others*, I am beyond excited to share what I've learned so that you too can experience the biggest, grandest, most unconditional love you can imagine. This book is not just about romantic love, it's about all sorts of love: parental love, platonic love, and even love for humanity in general. You deserve to feel more loved than you've ever felt before, and not only is it *possible for you*, it's also *up to you*. I'll be sharing exactly how you can take charge of the relationships you're co-creating in Part 3.

In Part 4, we'll address how you can implement what you've learned and cultivate an authentic, loving, and intimate romantic relationship while also improving all the other relationships in your life.

In this book, you will learn how to **create "fuck yes" relationships**. This means that your relationship *just feels so good*, you feel safe and accepted and loved. In practice this looks like:

- Maintaining respect and connection even during difficult conversations

- Leaning into challenges with love and curiosity

- Choosing yourself with unwavering passion and confidence

- Growing through difficult times, rather than running from them

What if you're currently in a relationship that doesn't quite *feel so good*? Does it mean it's doomed? Absolutely not! With the knowledge and tools provided in this book, you can transform your current experience into a "fuck yes."

If you're reading this book, I know that you are either stuck in or recovering from a relationship that leaves/left you feeling lonely and less than. *Firstly, I want to send you so much love.* I know how absolutely dire things can look from that vantage point. I hope you feel the energetic embrace I am sending straight from my heart to yours.

Secondly, I want you to know that one way or another, **the relationship of your dreams is possible.**

For me, it meant releasing what was not meant for me so that what truly WAS meant for me could find its way to me. It meant clarity on what I actually wanted and framing that in a positive way—something to move towards, rather than away from. For some of you, it might be as simple as changing your perspective. Questioning **why you see things the way you do**, understanding **why you respond the way you often do**, and exploring **why you feel the way you do** will shed some light on a lot of the challenges you are seeing played out inside your relationships. This book aims to unpack that in a way that will empower you to finally create the relationship you desire, regardless of where you're starting out.

Regardless of whether you believe your dream relationship is possible, I've got you. Inside this book you'll find perspective shifts, strategies and practical resources that, when put into practice, have the potential to transform every last one of your relationships from the inside out.

The more you love yourself, the more love you can receive and amplify. Radical self-acceptance leads to a deeper experience of love and quality of life in general. You can take control of how you see the world and what you experience, and you can create a new reality. You can change the world by loving yourself.

You are the executive producer of your life, and you can change the storyline if you choose to. Scratch what's not working and give it another go. If you feel like your current reality isn't quite congruent with your desired one, observe and adjust, just like I did.

A number of years ago, I felt trapped in an unhealthy and unhappy marriage. I spent all of my energy putting up a tough front to the outside world, all the while I was crumbling with insecurity about my marriage on the inside. I was living under the strain of constant anxiety, and I had moments where I was unable to see the light. All I could see was darkness and loneliness. I questioned often whether it was possible to ever get myself to a better place. Many times, I resigned myself to the life I had chosen.

I felt completely stuck in my relationship, unsure of which direction to take. To escape the overwhelming emotions, I filled my evenings with work and outings, even though I was exhausted and would have much rather stayed home. I joined sports teams and participated in multiple regular running groups, finding solace in the guise of "healthy" activities in an effort to avoid being alone with my thoughts.

Coffee, lunch, dinner, and any-time-of-the-day-drinks with friends became welcome distractions. I knew that if I had too much time to myself, I would end up *spiraling into a whirlwind of negative thoughts and emotions*, so I kept a full social calendar. I even attempted countless new hobbies (loom knitting, anyone?). I'd have done anything to keep my mind away from the turmoil within.

In my search for escape, I buried myself in Netflix shows, immersing myself in distant "worlds" to avoid facing my own reality. In fact, I remember watching the entirety of *Gossip Girl*—all 121 episodes—within a single calendar month, a feat I was both simultaneously proud and ashamed of.

The truth was, while I was utterly exhausted, all of this busyness provided an important "benefit"—it helped me avoid confronting the real issue: My relationship was on the rocks, and I had no idea whether it could be salvaged or not.

Over the years I had collected countless stories about what a relationship "should" be and was questioning where I had gone wrong. I had bought into the notion that your special someone was meant to "complete you," yet I was still waiting for my knight in shining armor to show up and save the day. I had accepted the idea that relationships ought to be "50/50," but I couldn't understand why it felt like I was carrying 110% of the emotional load. I had believed the many people who insisted marriage was "really difficult," and difficulties abounded, eager to confirm this belief.

As you can imagine, I was irritable, impatient, and disappointed—outward signs of the deep sadness and fear I was avoiding. The uncertainty around the future created massive amounts of anxiety, and my endless activities kept me in a constant state of overwhelm. As long as I continued to avoid truly facing myself, I continued to cultivate greater resistance to the things I told myself I "didn't want," along with a greater attachment to the things I "did want." What I failed to see then was that my avoidance was a misguided attempt at evading my fears, yet **it was this very resistance that was keeping me perpetually stuck** in fear based living patterns.

It was during this time that I had an appointment with my psychologist in which she asked me to create a list of things that "Christy" wanted in a relationship. Naturally, I began to tell her all of my grievances—all of the things I undoubtedly *did not want*. I did *not* want someone who spoke down to me, made me feel less than, ugly and unwanted, or like I would never have a hope in the world of being someone who is successful or valued. On and on I went with the list of things I did *not* want.

My therapist wasn't having any of it. As I continued to air my frustrations, she pressed me to think differently (one of the reasons I liked her, she really challenged my BS!)... What did I really *want*? What did I really *need*?

I honestly didn't even know who I was—how could I make this list? I had long resigned myself to being "just-a-mom" and had basically given up having my own desires outside of motherhood. I had a habit of complaining and I was so used to running away from the things I didn't want, that I had no familiarity with running towards what I *did* desire. I had a really hard time even just expressing the small things that I wanted for myself.

Selfish. This word had been thrown my way so often that I had started to internalize it as truth! As a mother of three growing boys, building a wellness business, and genuinely connecting with people in many circles, I finally began to question: *Was it actually selfish to desire happiness? Success? Peace? Love? Was it selfish to have my own desires and go after them?*

It was when I began to really question *my own beliefs* that things really started to shift.

When I began to question the beliefs that I had accepted—the sum of past experiences, my educational experience, my relational experiences, and the words of others accepted and internalized—**I started to learn more about ME**.

I was so over feeling unhappy. I was so over being lonely in my marriage. I was so over constantly walking on eggshells and putting on the best performance I could in an effort to make it all work. All of the efforting (and the mental stress of trying to avoid stepping on any hidden landmines) had me feeling burned out and lost. Although it took me a hot minute, eventually I learned that it doesn't have to be that way. *I learned that I deserved an epic relationship. And so do you!*

So, with the help of my therapist, I boldly claimed that which I desired, by making a list of all of the qualities I felt were important in a healthy relationship and ideal partner. I still have this list today, and I am beyond grateful that not that long after writing this list I met my dream partner. The one who hit *every quality on that list and then some.*

Today, I have the kind of relationship I once thought only existed in movies: a relationship built on wholeness, trust, and vulnerability. I am proud to have built a relationship where we can both show up exactly as we are, messy parts and all. But I didn't get here by accident. I got here by doing the work I'm about to share with you.

I will truly be forever grateful that I took the time to question my own thoughts and beliefs, and to explore them for the benefit of my future self. Reflecting back, a part of me can't help but wonder if things could have been different if I had known then what I know now. *Would I have avoided the pain, the struggle, the conflict, and all the attempts to avoid it?* The tears, the harsh words, the cold shoulders, the assumptions, the expectations, and the judgments? Would I have missed out on the cracking wide open, the expansion, the leap into the unknown, the hopes, the dreams, and the desires?

But the conclusion I have come to is that it doesn't matter. **There is no beginning and there is no end, it all just *is*.** Without experiencing all of it, I would not be here now, shaped into the person I have become. I wouldn't have the capacity to love as deeply and fully as I do now. I wouldn't understand and accept myself and humanity in the same way I do now. I wouldn't see the same infinite possibilities that I do now.

Looking back, it has all been a great gift—the best gift I could have been given, in fact. Embedded within its ugly crumbling exterior, it held the key understandings that I needed in order to create this incredible life right here. For that, I will be forever grateful. All the pain, struggle, conflict, and tears have played a part in shaping me into who I am today.

And it is only because I have been through my own "stuck" phase that I am now able to share my findings with you. After having navigated my way **from stuck to unstuck**, I am bursting to tell you all about my experience with love and how love itself transformed my life from the inside out. My desire is that this book will be a roadmap which helps to guide the next chapters in your story, transforming your life and love too.

My current relationship is not perfect. We still have our challenges and disagreements; but we have learned to navigate them in a healthy and constructive way, using the tools and techniques that I will be sharing in this book. We have a deep sense of mutual respect and admiration, and we genuinely enjoy spending time together, whether it's going on adventures or simply cuddling up on the couch. I am so grateful to have found a partner who shares my values and supports me in my growth and evolution as a person. And I am excited to share the insights and lessons that I have learned along the way.

The tools and insights I share in this book aren't just "nice ideas,"—they are proven methods that have transformed my relationships. I've noticed life-changing shifts in the relationships with my partner, my kids, my ex, my friends, my clients, my neighbors, and even strangers. They've revolutionized my relationship with food, my body, money, and the world at large. These principles have changed the lives of many—the only question is, will yours be next? If you're ready to experience the love you deserve, this book is the tool you need.

Are you ready? Let's begin.

> *"It becomes understood that happiness is not dependent on circumstances being exactly as we want them to be, or on ourselves being exactly as we'd like to be. Rather, happiness stems from loving ourselves and our lives exactly as they are, knowing that joy and pain, strength and weakness, glory and failure are all essential to the full human experience."*
>
> Kristin Neff

Part 1

Perspective is Everything

"The curious paradox is that when I accept myself just as I am, then I can change."
Carl Rogers

CHAPTER ONE

An Identity Problem

As I sat there, listening to my friend vent about her husband's socks scattered across the living room floor yet again, I couldn't help but feel a pang of envy. *Pfft! If only my problems were as minor as some stinky socks,* I thought with a huge internal eye roll. I faced far more significant challenges.

If it were MY socks on the floor, it would undoubtedly be an issue, I thought. I had always held myself to impossibly high standards, constantly striving to meet an ever-growing set of expectations, yet somehow always falling short. When I perceived a critical remark or disapproving look (sometimes reading into innocent comments), it seemed to trigger a defensive reaction within me. The fear of *never being good enough* seemed to cast a shadow on my every move.

My friend, I know that you're feeling frustrated or stuck, disconnected, unappreciated, not good enough, or even resentful when it comes to love and relationships. I want you to know that you're not alone in your struggles.

I've been there too. Let me share my experience:

Nearly every interaction felt like an attack, highlighting each and every one of my perceived inadequacies and confirming that my overwhelming fears of not measuring up were true. **I longed for a partner that would see me, appreciate me, and value me for who I truly was.** I wanted to experience a relationship safe haven, not feel like the subject of an ongoing audit (throwback to my professional accounting days!). The constant anxiety and overwhelm left me feeling disappointed and hopeless most of the time, yet somewhere deep down, I knew there had to be more to life and love than this constant struggle. The tiniest part within me somehow held onto the belief that I deserved better, and that happiness was possible.

Then, a pivotal shift occurred. My big AHA, or "holy shit" moment, if you will. It was in this pivotal moment when I realized that not only was I contributing to my current circumstances (*oof!*), but that I also had the power within to create new circumstances (*yay!*). It was then that I began to see that everything I had ever desired already existed within me, waiting to be rediscovered.

Maybe you find yourself wishing your partner would just change already. Perhaps within your relationships you struggle with communication, lack of intimacy, or passion. Maybe you and your partner fight over little things, you don't feel like you have much in common anymore, or you do not feel appreciated or respected. Perhaps you are waiting for the kids to grow up so that you can figure out your next steps. If you have ever had to "manage your partner's mood," by avoiding important issues, I understand why you are dissatisfied. If your partner tends to respond in erratic or volatile ways, it may feel much safer to keep your concerns to yourself. I can see why you have pushed your feelings down rather than expressing them. It's not safe to do otherwise.

On the other hand, you may be single and seeking a new love. Perhaps you are looking for a *forever relationship* so great that you feel inseparable from the other person, where without significant effort, you find there is constant harmony. A love where your partner considers your needs and is super romantic. And yet you are actually wondering what is wrong with you because you *still* haven't yet found this perfect love yet.

Regardless of where you are in your relationship journey, I'm here to share a perspective shift that might just change everything. *Almost certainly, the problem isn't what you think it is.*

Here's the truth bomb: You don't have a relationship problem—you have an identity problem.

While you may have been led to believe that your happiness depends on the quality of your relationships, the opposite is actually true: **the quality of your relationships reflects the happiness you have within.**

In this first part of the book, we'll take the time to look at the common denominator in all of your experiences: YOU. Does the very thought of taking responsibility make you angry, discouraged or upset? *Hold on*, don't throw this book across the room in frustration just yet! I know some of you have had some awful interactions with people who claimed to love you, and this is NOT about minimizing those experiences. You have never deserved to be mistreated, and this isn't about letting others off the hook for the things they've done to hurt you. What I am suggesting is a bit of a reset. Consider this: **the problem is... you've been looking to solve your relationship problems in the wrong places.**

This isn't about blaming yourself either. It is, however, about taking responsibility for your part in your relationships and recognizing that you have the power to make a positive change. You can't change anyone else, but you *can* change yourself. Starting with yourself is the best way to inspire change in your relationships and in the world around you.

Hard truths must be faced, but they come with opportunities for growth and improvement. In this section and throughout this book, you will step into your true power and discover what is possible. By changing yourself, you'll inspire others around you to change... and thus change your relationships from the inside out.

Let's Look Within

Consider these examples of common experiences and their internal cause:

Other's line-crossing behaviors are often permitted... due to your weak (or non-existent) boundaries

Feeling unworthy of love... often stems from a lack of self-love

Waiting for others to change before you do... reflects a lack of confidence in going after what you desire

Not knowing how someone really feels about you... is a result of not being vulnerable enough to ask the difficult questions or share your personal truths

Feeling as though we lack purpose or fulfillment... often occurs when we don't take the time for self-discovery

Not feeling like you belong... arises from a lack of self-acceptance

As we set off on this journey to find love, we must start with the most crucial foundation: yourself.

The foundation of self-love and acceptance must come first. If you can't love and accept yourself first, you cannot show others how you need to be treated. You'll be treated the way they think is best, which may or may not be aligned with what you want for yourself. So, my friend, are you ready to take responsibility for your part in the relationship and take the first step towards positive change?

As a mom, I know how crucial it is to take care of yourself. Your kids are watching. If you want them to love and accept themselves and embrace their unique gifts, you've got to do the same for yourself.

The amazing relationship you desire? It all starts with you.

As you embark on the journey of building a conscious relationship, it's important to keep in mind that **the foundation of any relationship is always the one we have with ourselves.** By cultivating a deep sense of love and acceptance within, we're able to enter relationships from a place of abundance and choice, rather than neediness or obligation.

But what exactly does it mean to have a healthy relationship with oneself? It starts with doing the inner work and taking a deep look within. This may involve:

- Facing uncomfortable truths about ourselves

- Examining our beliefs and values

- Identifying any self-defeating patterns or behaviors

As we become more aware of our inner workings, we can disentangle ourselves from that which no longer serves us. We create space for discovering more of what we truly desire in life and in love. And we become more confident in asking for what we need from others, free of fear of rejection or judgment.

Being authentically ourselves is key to creating a conscious relationship. To be authentically you means letting go of any expectations, people pleasing tendencies, or perfectionism that may be holding you back. If we are to create the loving relationships we desire, we must be curious, open, and accepting of ourselves and others. **By becoming more aware of who we are and what we want, we can create a massive shift in our experiences.** BTW—the miracle is in the perspective shift!

When we shift our perspectives, we create an opportunity for growth and exploration that is unmatched. We're able to embrace the beauty and messiness of life and approach it with a sense of wonder and curiosity. Only then can we see what we want to change (or embrace!) so that we can become truer versions of ourselves. Then we can be and show others who we really are and thus attract people who will enhance our lives, rather than compress them.

So, if you're feeling frustrated or stuck in your current relationship, remember that it all starts with you. By cultivating a foundation of self-awareness, radical self-love, and acceptance, you'll not only be able to create a more conscious and fulfilling relationship with your partner, but first with yourself. *And that, my friend, is where the magic fucking lies!*

Now, let's dive into some additional key perspectives and understandings about yourself and your humanity that will help you to see just why you've gotten into this mess in the first place.

CHAPTER TWO

You're Not Broken – You're Human

CONTRARY TO POPULAR BELIEF, healing isn't really about fixing yourself. If you're feeling like something is off when it comes to your relationships, this might surprise you: This doesn't mean that you're broken, *nor that the other person is the problem.* We are all complex human beings with a unique set of experiences and emotions. Healing is about learning to love and accept your wholeness—all parts of yourself—just as you are. Even if (especially when!) you're not yet where you'd like to be.

I have what some may consider a unique perspective on healing. I choose to look at being healed as simply operating from a state of wholeness. It's crucial to understand that *feeling stuck* isn't a sign that you're broken or need fixing. Instead, it's a powerful invitation to step into your next level of growth and evolution.

Stuck isn't necessarily a bad thing. Being stuck is simply the tension between where you are now and where you'd like to be. It's a call to expand, not because you're 'not good enough,' but because *it's your very nature* to continue growing and evolving. I extend an invitation to explore new possibilities and discover more of who you truly are.

Wholeness is your natural state. You are already complete, and healing is about reconnecting with that inherent wholeness, not trying to fix or change yourself. By approaching your journey from this perspective, you'll cultivate a deeper sense of self-acceptance and self-love, which will transform your relationships from the inside out.

In the journey towards healthier and more fulfilling relationships, self-acceptance is a central companion. The belief that one must be flawless to be worthy of love often originates from childhood conditioning, where messages about worthiness and perfection were absorbed. It's essential to recognize that true love isn't about finding a perfect partner but learning to accept an imperfect one, including embracing their flaws and quirks. However, *this journey of acceptance begins within us.*

If you've ever felt the need to apologize for your flaws and imperfections, it's time to replace that negative self-talk with some inner cheerleading. It's time to start embracing yourself wholeheartedly. You are magnificently human and there is beauty in every part of you (*yes, even THAT part*). The human experience is full of challenges, and self-compassion just might be the life changing ingredient that you've been missing.

This is where the groundbreaking work of Dr. Kristin Neff on self-compassion becomes particularly relevant. In her book *Self-Compassion: The Proven Power of Being Kind to Yourself,* Neff introduces the concept of self-compassion as a more effective alternative than self-criticism. She argues that **self-compassion involves treating yourself with the same kindness and understanding that you would offer a good friend**. This approach aligns perfectly with the idea of embracing your whole self, including your perceived flaws and imperfections.

Neff's research shows that practicing self-compassion can lead to greater emotional resilience, improved mental health, and more satisfying relationships. By incorporating these teachings, you can learn to acknowledge your struggles without harsh judgment, recognize the shared human experience of imperfection, and cultivate a gentle, supportive inner voice.

When you learn to love and accept your whole self, you will attract the love and acceptance you desire from others, and that includes your partner. So, let's take it one step further and start celebrating our quirks, our unique perspectives, our weaknesses-that-are-actually-strengths and our growth. Let's show up authentically and vulnerably in our relationships and finally let go of the fear of being judged or rejected. **It's time to stop apologizing and embrace the beautiful mess that is life and all of its imperfections. Besides, perfection is a mere illusion anyways.**

It's crucial to remember that your worthiness is not dependent on others' behaviors or opinions. Your value as a person is inherent and unchanging, regardless of how others treat you or what they think of you. By detaching your sense of self-worth from external validation, you create a solid foundation of self-love that isn't swayed by the actions or judgments of others. Ready to build your self-love? *Let's get your love on.*

Embracing Self-Love Mirror Exercise

One simple yet powerful tool that can aid you on your journey of self-acceptance and self-love is what I like to call the "Self-Love Mirror Exercise." It's a simple yet transformative practice that invites you to connect with yourself on a profound level. It's time to stop seeking external validation and looking for someone else to complete you. It's time to discover the magical wholeness within yourself.

The Mirror Exercise

Find a Quiet Space: To begin, find a quiet and comfortable space where you can be alone and undisturbed for a few minutes.

Stand in Front of a Mirror: Stand in front of a full-length mirror, or any mirror where you can see your reflection clearly.

Look Deeply into Your Eyes: Gaze into your own eyes in the mirror. Take a moment to really see yourself, acknowledging your presence and uniqueness.

Express Three Things You Love About Yourself: Now, here's where the magic happens. Verbally express three things that you genuinely love about yourself. These should be attributes, qualities, or aspects that are intrinsic to you, not related to how you relate to others or what you do for others. For example, you might say, "I love my creativity," "I love my resilience," or "I love my sense of humor." (Remember, this isn't about perfection or ego-boosting; it's about recognizing and appreciating the beautiful aspects of yourself that make you who you are.)

Accept Your Imperfections: As you engage in this exercise, embrace the idea that you are perfectly imperfect. You don't need to change anything about yourself to be whole. Your perceived flaws are part of what makes you unique and human.

Say I Love You: While gazing into your own eyes, tell yourself "I love you." Feel free to use this opportunity to tell yourself any other affirmations you need to hear.

Practice Regularly: Make this mirror work a part of your daily routine or ritual, or use it whenever you need a reminder of your wholeness. Over time, this practice can help you build self-love and self-confidence.

Note: This exercise may initially feel challenging or even uncomfortable, but that's perfectly okay. It's a journey of self-discovery and self-acceptance. As you continue to practice the self-love mirror exercise, you'll find that you're nurturing a deeper connection with yourself, allowing you to embrace your wholeness.

Remember, you are already complete, and by loving and accepting yourself fully, you're well on your way to creating healthier and more fulfilling relationships from the inside out.

CHAPTER THREE

Duality

We live in a world built upon duality—the idea that everything in life has *two opposing forces that create balance*. Up and down, big and small, good and bad, and so on. For something to exist, there must also be "nothing"—something that does not exist. To define our experience of something, we must have the language to describe it and a reference point or some criteria to be met. For example, in order for us to have a reference point for "big," we must also understand what "small" is. The truth is none of these descriptors are absolute—they all exist on a spectrum.

Embracing duality within oneself can mean being able to recognize that **we are complex humans, capable of experiencing a multitude of emotions**—sometimes even seemingly conflicting emotions, simultaneously—without attaching our overall identity to any singular one. It means recognizing that *we simply ARE*—our identity is not limited to one-sided labels.

Duality in a relationship can mean balancing your needs with your partner's needs, finding the middle ground between holding on and letting go, and navigating the ups and downs of life together. We'll talk more about duality in relationships in Chapter 8 and in Part 2. Here it is important to understand how our own misguided beliefs can really trip us up, and with the propensity towards negativity and our all-too-efficient confirmation bias, we may not even notice where duality exists (and is created), based on our own beliefs. For example, something as simple as believing that you need someone else to "complete you" fosters codependency and a victim mentality, while at the same time, it is the very same underlying belief that is the reason for one's felt sense of loss of control.

It's easy to get caught up in the idea of right versus wrong, good versus bad, but the truth is, life is rarely so black and white. Instead, we must learn to embrace the gray areas and find balance in the duality of life.

Embracing duality when it comes to relationships means accepting that *different viewpoints can all have some truth to them*. It's like seeing things from multiple angles and realizing that everyone's perspective is valid in its own way. There's no need to argue about who's right or wrong because each person's truth is important. Trying to convince others they're wrong leads to judgment and conflict. However, when we embrace the idea that there can be many truths, it sets us free from that cycle and opens us up to understanding and acceptance.

Another common experience of duality in our thinking is the tendency to engage in "us versus them" or "for and against" mentalities. This **black-and-white thinking can create unnecessary divisions in our relationships and society at large.** By recognizing that life, nor humanity, are rarely so simple, we can move beyond these limiting perspectives. Instead of seeing situations as "us versus them," we can strive to understand different viewpoints and find common ground. This shift from oppositional thinking to a more inclusive mindset allows for greater empathy, cooperation, and mutual understanding in our relationships and communities.

It's important to recognize and accept the duality within yourself. You are not perfect, and that's okay. You have both positive and negative qualities, strengths and weaknesses, and embracing both aspects of yourself is essential for finding balance in your relationship.

In the highest sense, all experiences are rooted in either love or fear. Fear acts to keep you "safe" inside your comfort zone of familiar experiences—it feels restrictive and small. Love, on the other hand, is expansive and limitless. *You are not here to suffer.* In fact, quite the opposite! Remember, finding balance in the duality of life is not about choosing one extreme or the other, but rather finding the middle ground that allows you to live authentically and love deeply.

More to the point, **all experience simply 'is' until we label it and attach meaning to it.** There are no universal truths—all that exists *simply 'is'* until it is perceived and judged. It is *your perception* which creates your personalized version of "reality," and how *you* experience that which simply 'is.'

By recognizing and accepting this duality first within yourself you will begin to find more balance, not only in your relationship with yourself, but in your entire experience of reality. It's okay to have differences, conflicts, and challenges as you strive to understand yourself and your values—it's how you navigate them (along with the stories you're telling yourself) that ultimately determines your strength and your understanding of what makes you "you." This also means being able to hold all of the experiences, "good" or "bad," as simply part of the magnificently *messy fucking beautiful human experience.*

CHAPTER FOUR

You Are Creating Your Reality With Your Thoughts

NOTHING HAPPENS IN YOUR perceived reality that did not first originate as a thought. Your messy fucking beautiful thoughts, as well as the not-so-beautiful ones, are incredibly powerful, and this means that if you are not aware of your thoughts, you may be creating experiences that *you do not want*. It is this powerful skill of thought creation that you must harness in order to intentionally create less of the experiences you don't want and *more of the experiences you do want in your life and in your relationship.*

Over time, repeated thoughts become your beliefs, and these beliefs in turn create your expectations. Your beliefs and expectations directly shape your experience of reality—whether you are aware of this or not—so, it's important to get curious about how you might shift your thoughts if you desire to create an experience more congruent with what you truly want. For example, if you believe that your relationship is always going to be difficult, then your actions and behaviors will align with that belief and expectation, making it a self-fulfilling prophecy. However, **if you shift your thoughts**

and beliefs to focus on what you do want, you can create an experience of reality that is more aligned with your desires.

Let's take a look at this thought creation in action with an example. Say you believe an interaction with your partner will turn into a disagreement. With this assumption in mind, you will most likely approach these conversations with a defensive attitude. By armoring up and expecting a battle, you in fact create the ideal atmosphere for conflict. This defensiveness itself will form the basis for which your body language, your words and your responses will be chosen, and this will often even result in your defending yourself *before there is an attack*. By assuming and expecting an attack, you have in effect positioned yourself for battle, and often, a battle is what you will create through your expectant words and actions. On the other hand, if you were to approach your partner with the assumption that an enjoyable conversation is imminent, you will be better positioned to respond to the actual experience before you, creating an opportunity for a truly meaningful exchange. **Not only are your own words and actions impacted by your expectation, the other person's words and actions will be too.**

Why We Tell Ourselves the Stories We Do

The stories we tell ourselves about our relationships and the world around us don't just appear out of thin air. They're deeply rooted in our childhood experiences and the lessons we learned as we grew up. Our inner child, that part of us that holds our earliest memories and emotions, plays a significant role in shaping these narratives.

For instance, if you grew up in a household where conflict was frequent and intense, your inner child might have learned that disagreements are scary and dangerous. As an adult, this can manifest as an expectation that any serious conversation with your partner will turn into a fight. This expectation then influences your behavior, causing you to approach discussions defensively, even when there's no real threat.

These early childhood experiences affect our mental filter, or what psychologists call our "schema." This schema acts like a lens through which we view all our experiences, often distorting our perception of reality.

For example:

- If you experienced neglect as a child, you might develop a schema that tells you "I'm not important." As an adult, this could lead you to misinterpret your partner's busy schedule as a sign that they don't value you, even when that's not the case.

- If you were often criticized as a child, you might develop a schema of "I'm not good enough." This could cause you to be overly sensitive to any feedback from your partner, perceiving even constructive comments as attacks.

These schemas or stories can distract us from the truth of reality, causing us to *react to our past traumas rather than the present moment*. The example of expecting a fight and coming up defensive illustrates this perfectly—you're not reacting to what's actually happening, but rather to what your childhood experiences have taught you to expect.

Another example of your beliefs and expectations altering your perception of reality is a commonly used one. You've likely heard this one before—and probably experienced this very phenomenon—as it's a great example of how your inner focus can alter your perception of reality. The premise is this: **what you seek is what you will find**.

Imagine you've just purchased a new car. Let's assume for fun that it's a Volkswagen Beetle—yellow!—like the make and model of my favorite amongst the vehicles I've owned.

Prior to purchasing this car, I had seen perhaps five of them on the road, but after I purchased that car, they were EVERYWHERE! It is the same for all of us: by purchasing a particular car you shift your focus, altering the fancy pants filter in your brain (called the Reticular Activating System, or RAS for short). So, after buying a fabulous yellow VW Bug, they are seemingly everywhere you look! Are there suddenly ten times more yellow Bugs on the road? Probably not. You're simply witnessing the power of your RAS in action, bringing into your awareness that which is now familiar. In order to get this filter working to help you experience the reality you desire, rather than the reality that is merely a reflection of your familiar past, you've got to *get intentional about those thoughts and beliefs you allow in on repeat.*

And as frustrating as it may be to experience this often-incredibly-biased filter, your mind is simply doing its job: keeping you safe. Your RAS is set to seek out that which is congruent with your existing beliefs, but you don't have to let it run amok (we'll talk more about this in Chapter 6: Who Are You Really?).

But Christy, you might ask, *why is it so hard to make this change?*

There is a reason that you struggle to make lasting change, and it's not because your partner or parent-in-law is an asshole, it's because *your mind can be an asshole*. Your brain is a high-powered machine filtering through something like a gazillion potential data points per second and choosing which if any data points are relevant and necessary to your immediate current experience. The reality is that there is a huge amount of information available from which our brains must filter—in fact the common belief is that the amount of data points is somewhere in the tens of millions of pieces of data per second. With so much available data, I sometimes wonder: if our brains had to process it all, might they just explode?

Thankfully, our RAS exists to help prevent such an explosion, and to help filter into our conscious awareness the tiny fraction of data which our brain can process (without exploding). Research shows this to be significantly less than 100 bits of information per second, and even without doing any fancy math here, we can see that this means there are a lot of data points that our RAS is filtering out.

This filtering process is heavily influenced by our childhood experiences and the stories we've internalized. If your childhood taught you to be wary of others' intentions, your RAS might prioritize information that confirms this belief, even in situations where it's not warranted. This is why awareness of our inner narratives is so crucial—it allows us to consciously challenge and change these filters.

So, what does it filter in? In a nutshell, it filters in the things it believes are most important to you and that which is a match for your desires: things that are known and familiar, things that make sense, and things that you expect to see. Basically, what gets filtered in is what matches your expectations and assumptions, much like an automatic confirmation bias. If you're looking for and expecting difficulties, guess what you're going to see? That's right, difficulties.

Without intentional new input, your RAS will continue to filter out what is deemed unnecessary and create a personalized lens of perception for the creation of your reality. This will even run on autopilot with no additional input necessary. In autopilot mode, this filter comprises your past thoughts, experiences, emotions and memories. Basically, it's operating to *recreate your past over and over.*

It's no wonder you find yourself stuck living a perpetual Groundhog Day. You ARE stuck in a perpetual experience of, well, the same old shit. And the longer you live your life on autopilot, experiencing, thinking and feeling the same things, these less than desirable neural pathways in your brain become more deeply ingrained, creating bigger and bigger ruts that can eventually seem impossible to get out of. I recommend learning the Spiral Stopper Method taught in my book, *Unstuck for Women,* to get past this type of overthinking. This method can help you eliminate thought and emotional spirals that lead to overwhelm and anxiety. The book provides tools that can help you to not only stop the spiral, but also to create the space required for conscious creation.

Our inner thoughts and dialogue can either negatively or positively impact our ability to be authentic and vulnerable in relationships. Arguing with your mind and with the reality of "what is" is a waste of your precious time and energy. Instead, surrender to what is and allow yourself just to be here, now. **The choice is yours to make.** Remember, you have the power to shift your reality by shifting your thoughts and beliefs, so it's crucial to choose them wisely and consciously. If you believe relationships can be easy, you can actually create the possibility of this experience for yourself. Once you understand that you are not your thoughts, the next step is to realize that *you are the observer of your thoughts.* This shift in perspective allows you to see your thoughts, emotions, and even your body as part of *the flow of your human experience,* rather than being the essence of your identity. Let's explore that now.

CHAPTER FIVE

You Are the Observer

WHEN WE ARE HEAVILY identified with our thoughts, emotions, or body, we can confuse things that only contribute to our identity with the whole of who we are. For example, if you believe, based on your thoughts, that you are a failure, this makes it so in your experience, but this does not make it true. We humans far too often conflate our mistakes ("missed takes!") with failure, concluding that we ourselves are a failure when this is the furthest thing from the truth. In fact, the *most successful people on the planet will tell you that they make many mistakes, and they make them often*! What makes them truly successful is their perspective on these missed takes and their willingness to continue making them, knowing they are a necessary part of success.

Having thoughts is part of being human, but it's important to realize that accepted thoughts about ourselves form our identity. If we accept and agree with our negative thoughts, they can become beliefs about ourselves, which can quickly lead to a case of *mistaken identity*.

You are not your thoughts!

Our thoughts can trigger an emotional response—make us happy or sad or concerned or angry. When we believe that our emotions define us, we can easily confuse our grumpy mood with being a grumpy person. The mood is of course temporary, yet we can end up taking on this experience as a permanent feature of our identity, labeling and limiting ourselves based on something that was only ever one experience of many.

You are not your emotions!

When we assume that our body is *us*, we take on labels such as short/tall, male/female, healthy/unhealthy, none of which truly define who we are as a human. The truth is, we are far more than any of these limiting concepts.

You are not a body!

We will further explore *who we really are* in the next chapter, but for now, it is important to know that you always have the power to observe your thoughts, emotions, and body as separate entities from your true self (you may understand this as 'Self', High Self, your Spirit or your Soul). You can observe your thoughts as they come and go—and as a conscious creator, you have the power to choose the ones that support your desired experience. Your thoughts can be incredibly powerful, but you don't have to let them control you. For example, once during a walk I was consciously reflecting on how great I felt while outside moving my body, when in popped the thought, *You know what'd be great? Chocolate cake!* (Thanks, asshole mind. *Some fucking chocolate cake.* Seriously. The audacity!)

Now, I knew this thought was not me because I had just been reflecting on my positive health choice. Luckily, I get to choose what I do with my thoughts, so I chuckled to myself about the absurdity of the thought in that context and continued my walk. Just because I'd had the thought, did not mean I needed to stop taking the healthy actions I had consciously chosen. Without our judgments, our thoughts carry little weight; they can easily float away as quickly as they came into our mind, creating space for us to *select those thoughts that support our desired experience instead.* By getting curious about your thoughts and shifting them to align with what you truly want, you can intentionally create a more fulfilling reality.

The same goes for your emotions. In short, emotions are our physical experience of *energy in motion.* This energy in motion essentially acts as an inner barometer, alerting us to that which feels "good" for us and that which does not. Often, our emotions can be confused with or inflated by the stories we are telling ourselves, taking the beliefs and judgments we have about the situation and applying them to the emotion we are experiencing. I call this story-telling process *the creation of thought-feelings.* Fortunately, these thought-feelings can be treated in the same manner as we have treated our thoughts above. In just the same way, you are not your emotions; you are merely the observer of them.

As a conscious creator, when you physically experience your emotions, you have the power to choose which thoughts and stories you attach to them. Without your added meanings, your emotions simply exist as information and typically pass very quickly. By objectively examining your emotions and allowing them to flow through you, you can feel them without getting trapped in the spiral of emotions and thought-feelings. By freeing yourself from this spiral, you gain clarity and can make more intentional choices.

Exercise in Mindful Meditation: Stepping into the Role of the Observer

As you explore the idea that you are not your thoughts, emotions, or body, here's a simple exercise to help you connect with your true self. The goal is to step into the role of the observer, taking a step back from the constant activity of your mind, emotions, and body.

1. **Find a quiet space.** Sit comfortably in a chair or on the floor, with your back straight and hands resting in your lap. Close your eyes if that feels comfortable.

2. **Take three deep breaths.** Inhale deeply through your nose, filling your lungs with air, and exhale slowly through your mouth. Feel the physical sensations of your breath entering and leaving your body.

3. **Become aware of your body.** Notice how your body feels—its weight on the chair or floor, the feeling of your clothes against your skin. You are observing your body without judgment, simply acknowledging its presence.

4. **Notice your thoughts.** Allow your thoughts to come and go *without engaging with them*. If a thought pops up, like "I'm bored" or "I wonder what's for dinner," observe it, and then gently let it pass, as if you are watching clouds drift across the sky. *You are not your thoughts; you are the one who notices them.*

5. **Observe your emotions.** If any emotions arise, like frustration or calmness, notice them too. See them

as passing waves. Allow yourself to feel without attaching meaning or judgment. Just let the emotion be there for a moment and *observe how it changes.*

6. **Return to your breath.** If your mind wanders or you find yourself getting caught up in a thought or emotion, gently return your focus to your breath. Inhale, exhale, and notice how the air feels as it moves through your body.

By simply observing your body, thoughts, and emotions in this way, you begin to understand that you are much more than them. This brief pause helps you reconnect with the truth that you are the observer, and as a conscious creator, you can choose which thoughts and emotions to engage with. You are not controlled by them—they are just experiences passing through.

Feel free to practice this exercise whenever you need a reminder that you are so much more than your thoughts, emotions, and body. **You are the observer.**

You have the power to choose how you will experience your life while in this human body. You are a conscious creator—and you are so much greater than the meatsuit you're currently exploring life in. According to the most modern theories of quantum physics, *you are energy,* and that energy expands beyond your flesh and bones. Your body is made up of energy—which I like to imagine as *love*—vibrating fast enough that our senses interpret it as solid. The reality is that you are mostly made up of empty space between particles.

You can learn to love and appreciate your vessel, using your body's strengths and gifts to create the highest and best experience for yourself. **Even your perceived flaws are spectacularly designed just for you** and can often contain gifts and lessons for you and your highest self.

By taking a step back and putting yourself in the role of the observer, you can more clearly see where your identity and experience have been created by your thoughts, emotions and your physical body.

And now that you can see more clearly what and who you are *not*, it's time to look at *who you really are*.

Chapter Six

Who You Really Are

You are a human being, not a human doing. Your superpower lies in being *you*, not in what you *do* or who you are *with*. There is actually nothing that *you need to do*. Rather, **your purpose is simply to create the experiences that you desire.** Learning to *be* is part of what creates authenticity. It helps you to know who you are.

Maybe you feel like you've been doing everything to make your relationship work, but it's still not where you want it to be and you're feeling frustrated and disappointed. You're experiencing the gap between your current reality and your desired one and assuming your problem is that *you're not measuring up.*

But what if it's not?

As I discovered in my own journey, the key to transforming our relationships often lies within ourselves, not in trying to change our partners or circumstances.

As young children, we all experienced even small disappointments in a more life or death kind of way. In those moments where our safety or security was brought into question, we felt the tension within and, in our attempt to understand what was causing this tension, we created a conundrum. We were faced with the option of assuming our caregivers were incompetent (which would be a huge problem since we needed them to survive) or, alternatively, the possibility that there is something wrong with us. But what if neither of these conclusions are actually true? What if neither of you were bad or wrong, and both of you were simply doing the best you could with the resources and understanding you each had at the time. And furthermore... **What if that common misunderstanding has actually gotten in the way of understanding who you really are, all this time?**

When we go through life assuming there is something innately wrong with us, we end up creating a lot of suffering for ourselves. The truth is, blame is irrelevant, and the situation just *is*. However, the way you have interpreted it and assigned meaning will determine how you experience this particular encounter. Here's the real rub: **Your worth doesn't depend on what you can do for someone else, it comes from within you.** You've been duped to believe there was something wrong with you and now you've gone through life thinking you're bad and wrong and there will never be enough, and nothing will ever get better... *and it has all been a lie.*

You are inherently worthy simply for being *you*, and there is always more happiness, more peace, more fun, more love, and more success to experience. In fact, these qualities are what you are here to experience, and none of it exists outside of *you*. Yet perhaps at this point you may not even quite know what brings you happiness, peace, fun, love and success, and that's okay too. When you focus first on being, you will find your path.

Ultimately, there are no right or wrong ways to experience life, only what is correct (or not) *for you*. This means you simply cannot get it wrong! There are no experiences that don't ultimately serve your growth in some way or another. You either have your intended experience, or you learn what didn't work. Phew! What a load off.

Learning what doesn't work for you is actually a wonderful gift, pointing you towards what does or will work for you.

Go Deeper

If you're ready to dive deeper into discovering your true self and how that impacts your relationships, I'd encourage you to check out my program *Love Reimagined*. This in-depth exploration will guide you through the process of cultivating self-awareness, radical self-love, and acceptance—the foundation for building the relationships you truly desire.

Getting to know yourself at a deeper level will help you to see more clearly what experiences you are here to create for yourself. Discovering, for example, what your key values are, can help you to identify which experiences and relationships are—and are not!—a match with much more ease. Experimenting with different types of experiences can help you to discern both your superpowers and your interests. Learning more about your unique self will help you to express yourself in a way that feels correct for you, freeing yourself from the shackles of following society's epically arbitrary "rules." **Self-discovery is a process of stripping away** that which is *not* you, much like the sculptor chisels away at the clay until they have revealed the masterpiece within. Unlearning the beliefs, conditioning and fear that have kept you from seeing the truth of who you are can be a truly life changing experience. The more you get to know who you are, the easier it is to create the experiences you most desire—first by *being* in the desired state, and *then* taking action.

So, you've stripped away all the labels and beliefs you've picked up along the way—*what's left*? At your core, **you are pure loving consciousness.** When you learn how to tap into this infinite resource within yourself, you will no longer need to rely on external sources (or other people), freeing up a lot of your time and energy seeking things that you never needed in the first place. With all this newfound spaciousness, *enter the practice of being.*

You have the power to create the experiences you desire—it starts with the decision that *it is yours.* You have the power to create the relationship you desire, by being true to who you are and creating experiences that align with your heart's desires (AKA your purpose). Don't let your fears or doubts stop you from experiencing the best that life has to offer. Unconditional love is within you, ready to be discovered.

You have the ability to create relationships in which everyone can be their fully authentic selves, and it starts with accepting yourself just as you are. *Your first and most important relationship is with yourself.* If you want happiness, peace, fun, love, and success in a relationship, you don't have to find it, you have to *be* it. The key to authentic expression is feeling safe enough to allow what you feel, even when faced with the discomfort of your doubt and fear. Being vulnerable is actually a superpower, it's time now for you to claim it.

CHAPTER SEVEN

Vulnerability is Your Superpower

Do you feel like being vulnerable means being weak? Do you avoid sharing your feelings because you're afraid of being dismissed or judged? I understand how that feels. I used to feel the same. But then I learned something that changed my perspective completely: *vulnerability is actually a superpower.*

Think about it. **Deep love requires vulnerability.** You can't have a deeply intimate connection with someone without opening yourself up to the possibility of being hurt. However, it's also important to note that not everyone has the capacity to hold a safe space for your emotions, so it's important for you to recognize who you feel safe with and who you don't.

Fortunately, even if you can't find anyone who can hold space for your emotions, you can still get started by being vulnerable with yourself. To do that, you need to create safety and acceptance *for yourself.* The beautiful bonus to this is that when you know your own truths and who you are, what others think or say has far less impact on you. I call this unstoppable self-confidence *being unfuck-withable!*

In addition to being vulnerable with sharing your emotions, it's time to stop hiding and minimizing your truths, longings, and dreams. **You don't have to make others happy by avoiding sharing your truths–because their happiness is not up to you.** By stuffing down and avoiding your own stuff, you're taking away the only happiness that you can create—*your own.*

Exercise in Vulnerability with Self: Embracing Your Superpower

Time and time again I have noticed that leading by example is the fastest way to create massive transformation and impact! Happiness is contagious, and by creating your own happiness, you'll also inspire others with it.

As you start seeking safe spaces where you can be vulnerable, you can start today by simply being more vulnerable with yourself. Here are a few places to start:

1. Spend time reflecting on your thoughts and consider whether they serve you. Are they helping you move towards your goals and desires, or are they holding you back? When you can identify negative self-talk or limiting beliefs, you can start to challenge them and replace them with more empowering thoughts.

2. Consider your beliefs and whether they are serving you or holding you back. Do you believe in abundance or scarcity? Do you believe in your own worthiness and ability to create the life you desire? When you examine your beliefs, you can start to shift them towards ones that empower you.

3. Allow yourself to feel all feelings, even the uncomfortable ones. When you acknowledge and accept your emotions, you can start to process them and move on. And when you're not constantly suppressing or avoiding your feelings, you can be more present in your relationships and in your life.

4. Consider who you are and who you desire to become. What are your values, your passions, your strengths? What kind of person do you want to be? When you have a clear vision of your ideal self, it becomes easier to make choices and take actions that align with that vision.

5. Allow yourself to dream without limiting yourself. What would you do if you knew you couldn't fail? What kind of life would you create for yourself? When you give yourself permission to dream big, you open new possibilities and can start taking steps towards making those dreams a reality.

Radical self-acceptance (accepting your flaws and all) is crucial when it comes to creating relationships in which you feel completely accepted. This sense of acceptance must emanate from within if we are to experience it in our external reality in relationship with others.

We will of course be exploring these themes in greater depth throughout the book, but the key thing here is simply to ask yourself these intentional questions, and then remain quiet long enough to hear your answers within.

Vulnerability with Others

As you gain confidence being vulnerable with yourself, you can then begin practicing vulnerability in relationships with others. We aren't meant to do life alone, so we must be willing to communicate honestly and openly in order to be heard and build connections.

It is not selfish to communicate your needs nor to desire peace, happiness, and love yet you must learn to ask for what you need and believe you can and will have it. You can learn to express your truths as needed to others with kindness, as we will learn in Part 3.

But Christy, being vulnerable is so scary! Yes, vulnerability comes with risk *but so does fear.* However, love has the potential to make your life better, while fear will only make it worse. I mean, be really fucking honest with yourself: Have you ever once made things better with your worry, fear, and negativity?

Neither have I.

In fact, neuroscience research has proven again and again that when you ruminate on fearful and worrisome things, you tend to create that which you fear most. However, **when you ruminate on love and peace, you manifest more love and peace.**

When you learn to create the love and safety that you need for yourself, you will realize that you *never needed to measure up to anyone else's expectations in the first place.* It's time to stop unintentionally sabotaging yourself and keeping yourself stuck.

When you choose to place your faith in love, it has the power to change your life for the better. So don't let the fear of vulnerability hold you back—embrace it as a superpower and start living your life authentically and fully.

As the saying goes:

"Be yourself; everyone else is already taken."
Oscar Wilde

CHAPTER EIGHT

The Relationship Paradox

PASSION AND SECURITY—THE SEEMINGLY paradoxical requirements for a healthy and happy relationship, one that goes the distance. But how the heck, you might wonder, can you navigate these seemingly opposing desires and create a relationship that is both safe *and* exciting?

Here is my answer: by holding space for **BOTH/AND.**

It's not a matter of choosing passion or security over the other; it's not *either/or*, but rather it's about creating harmony in the coexistence of *both* passion *and* security. Many believe that commitment and excitement are mutually exclusive (or worse, contradictory!), and end up settling for only one or the other. But what if that belief is not entirely true?

As we discussed previously in Chapter 3: Duality, life is seldom black and white; relationships are no different. The notion that passion and commitment must be mutually exclusive is a limiting belief we ought to challenge. Embracing the idea of *both/and* allows us to create relationships that are *both* safe *and* exciting.

Let's try on a different belief for a moment: What if it's possible to experience *both* security *and* butterflies in a relationship?

I'm here to tell you that it not only is possible, but actually quite achievable—*if you're willing to create it for yourself.* You can have the relationship of your dreams, when you choose to and take action to create it.

Duality within the context of a relationship also means embracing both the light and dark aspects of both your partner and you. It's important to acknowledge and accept both the positive and negative qualities of your partner and the relationship. **When two whole people come together?** *Pure magic!*

Consider Ella and Jake who met at a mutual friend's party and were immediately drawn to each other's energy. Their early relationship was electric—filled with passion, adventure, and an undeniable chemistry. However, as things began to progress, Ella felt an underlying anxiety about whether their excitement could translate into something lasting. Jake was more laid-back and valued stability over adventure, which left Ella feeling a bit disconnected at times. Instead of letting this disconnect drive them apart, they chose to embrace the *both/and* mentality.

To address this concern, Ella and Jake started having weekly check-ins where they would openly discuss their feelings, fears, and desires. During these conversations, they learned to appreciate their differences rather than view them as obstacles. Ella shared her need for adventure, while Jake expressed his desire for stability. Together, they found ways to incorporate spontaneity into their routine, like surprise weekend getaways, while also establishing rituals that fostered a sense of security, such as a weekly date night. This intentional effort not only deepened their emotional connection but also ignited a renewed sense of passion in their relationship. By understanding and valuing each other's needs, they were able to create a dynamic that balanced both safety and excitement—a true partnership based on the principles of the *both/and* approach.

Now of course this doesn't mean ignoring red flags or staying in a toxic situation. It means finding the balance between acknowledging the challenges and focusing on the positive aspects that make the relationship worth fighting for. When we replace *either/or* thinking (such as black or white, right or wrong, good or bad) with *both/and* thinking, we are able to experience both black *and* white *and* all of the colors in between—the full spectrum of the human experience!

So, how do we bridge this gap? **The journey to a fulfilling relationship, as always, begins with you.** By taking radical responsibility for yourself and actively living the life you desire, you create the conditions conducive to your ideal relationships.

All other relationships build upon the relationship you have with yourself—*if this is not solid, you WILL struggle unnecessarily.* It's important to note that you can work on both your relationship and yoursel at the same time, but working on the relationship only *without* working on yourself will most likely prove futile. Besides, if you're not happy with yourself, it's time to create something that *does* make you happy. **Once you're solid with yourself, you'll be solid with others too.**

Of course, "set it and forget it" doesn't work in relationships—it's crucial for both you and your partner to purposefully invest time and effort into connecting with each other regularly, free from distractions. By focusing your intentions and expanding your beliefs, you automatically open up greater possibilities and opportunities for experiencing the successful relationships you deserve, where passion and safety coexist and the love you've been seeking becomes a tangible reality.

It's time to create relationships that not only embrace the paradox and rewrite the rules, but ultimately will thrive on the beautiful interplay of passion and commitment. *Are you willing?*

Chapter Nine

Your Willingness

BEFORE WE DIVE INTO the strategies for moving past feeling stuck in your life and relationship, it is important to check-in and ask one extremely important question:

Are you willing and ready to experience more?

If your answer is a resounding "fuck yes," then you're in the right place because it's time to get unstuck in relationship!

When you are willing to embrace and eventually embody self-love and self-acceptance, you *will* see a shift in all of your relationship experiences. **Your willingness is a powerful force in your life.** What you tolerate can quickly become mediocrity or settling for less than you deserve. It's essential to remember that what we tolerate becomes the norm over time.

If you're unhappy with the current state of your relationship, know that you have the power to create a new reality. If you are looking for a new romantic partner, know that you deserve to have the relationship of your dreams, and you are amazing enough to make it happen.

But, if you're aware that you're unhappy and still choose to do nothing about it, that is also a choice. *Why not choose yourself this time?* You deserve to have a relationship that brings you joy and fulfillment, and it's time to make that happen. It's time to *decide it's yours.*

Congratulations! You've taken a monumental step in shifting your perspective and gaining clarity on what you truly desire in your relationships. This is no small feat, and it's important to celebrate the progress you've made in understanding the underlying patterns that shape your experiences.

In the next section, we'll focus on creating safety and getting in touch with your true self. You'll embark on a journey of self-discovery, exploring essential patterns like attachment styles, people pleasing tendencies, narcissism, codependency, and hyper independence. Recognizing and understanding these patterns will empower you to break free from limitations and step into a more authentic version of yourself.

You've got this, and I'm here for you.

Now that you have spent time becoming more aware of who you are and gaining perspective on the uniqueness of you, let's explore how to be the best version of yourself. In Part 2, you'll learn how to get unstuck so you can improve your relationship with yourself and co-create the types of relationships you deserve.

Part 2
Getting Unstuck

"Your task is not to seek for love, but merely to seek and find all the barriers within yourself that you have built against it."
Rumi

CHAPTER TEN

Get The Fuck Unstuck

READY TO BREAK FREE from the relationship quicksand and reclaim your fucking awesome self? It's time to get unstuck and create the love story you've always dreamed of!

In Part 1, we talked about the key perspective shifts that will allow you to reimagine love from a new perspective. Now that we've set the stage for understanding relationships, it's time to explore exactly how to get unstuck so that you can finally *be the healthy, loving partner with whom you want to spend your life.*

If you're feeling stuck in your relationship, you're not alone. Many people find themselves in common scenarios that leave them feeling trapped or unfulfilled:

1. Feeling Stuck in a Rut: You're tired of trying to improve your relationship without seeing any progress. You feel like the only one putting in effort, and you've given up hope of seeing real change. The constant struggle leaves you feeling unloved, unseen, and unappreciated. (This is exactly why we're here in Chapter 10: Get the Fuck Unstuck)

2. Putting Up a Tough Front: You've built a tough exterior to protect yourself from feeling vulnerable. You stopped sharing your feelings, asking for help, and expressing your dreams and desires. The fear of not measuring up and being judged keeps you constantly on guard, making it difficult to connect authentically with your partner. (We'll tackle this in Chapter 12: Feel to Heal, where we'll explore the importance of emotional expression and vulnerability)

3. The Busyness Trap: You find yourself busier than a mosquito at a nude beach! You take on extra work, join various groups and activities, and fill every spare moment to avoid facing the reality of your unhappy relationship. The constant busyness provides a false sense of control and distracts you from your deep sadness and fear. (We'll address this in Chapter 19: Balancing Energy and Creating Space, where we'll explore how to intentionally create time for your relationship)

4. Lack of Safety and Trust: You struggle to feel safe in your relationship and have difficulty trusting your own intuition. This leaves you feeling disconnected and unsure of how to move forward. (We'll explore this in Chapters 11: Creating Safety, 12: Feel to Heal, and 13: Trusting Your Intuition, where we'll discuss building a foundation of safety, healing emotional wounds, and reconnecting with your inner wisdom)

5. Complex Relationship Dynamics: You find yourself caught in patterns of codependency, people pleasing, or dealing with narcissistic behaviors. Perhaps you've become hyper independent as a way to protect yourself. These dynamics create imbalance and frustration in your relationships. (We'll dive into these topics in Chapters 15: Building Emotional Intelligence, 20: Ditch the People Pleasing Tendencies, 21: Codependency & Narcissism, and 22: Balancing Independence & Interdependence)

6. The Stay or Go Dilemma: You're facing the difficult decision of whether to stay in your relationship or leave. You feel torn between your commitment and your desire for happiness, unsure of which path to take. (We'll address this challenging crossroads in Chapter 23: Should I Stay, or Should I Go?)

Recognizing these patterns is the first step towards breaking free from them. But what if you could not only break free but also transform your relationships entirely?

This section of the book will guide you through a journey of self-love, acceptance, and personal growth that will help you build a solid foundation for healthy and fulfilling relationships, no matter which scenario you find yourself in.

Throughout Part 1, we'll address these challenges and more, providing you with tools and insights to:

- Create safety in your body and relationship

- Break the cycle of chronic stress and trauma

- Connect with your emotions and heal your inner child

- Trust your intuition and develop self-trust

- Give without expectations and let go of scorekeeping

- Become fully expressed by shedding masks of people pleasing and perfectionism

- Reclaim your power and step into your authentic self

By embracing these concepts and doing the work, you'll discover:

- A newfound sense of clarity and direction in your relationships

- The confidence to express your authentic self

- A deeper connection with your own needs and desires

- The ability to create relationships that support your growth and happiness

We'll start by discussing the importance of creating safety in your body and your relationship. We'll explore how chronic stress, and trauma can lead to living in survival mode and operating on autopilot, and *how you can break the cycle to consciously create your experiences*. We'll also look at the concept of working with your inner child, and how connecting with your emotions will help you heal and move forward.

Trusting your intuition is crucial to developing a healthy relationship with yourself and others, so we'll talk about ways to tune in to your inner barometer and how to learn to trust yourself (which is foundational to being able to trust others). We'll also explore the power of giving without expectations, letting go of scorekeeping, and how by creating a loving and balanced energy within yourself, you can transform your relationships.

Finally, we'll dive into how you can become fully expressed by shedding the patterns of people pleasing, perfectionism, and codependence. You will learn how to take back your power and step into the authentic, confident person you are meant to be—the version of you who has incredible relationships! By the end of this section, you'll have the tools and insights to get unstuck, ready to finally create the love and connection you deserve.

Are you ready to break free from the patterns holding you back and create the relationships you've always dreamed of? Let's dive in and discover the transformative power of getting unstuck!

Chapter Eleven

Creating Safety

Living in a state of survival mode for extended periods (very common in today's world) can leave you feeling unsafe in your day-to-day life. This can result in operating on autopilot, reliving a loop of past experiences, emotions, and thoughts that no longer serve you. In this state, you may find yourself *reacting rather than responding* to situations, leading to inappropriate behavior and strained relationships.

The first step towards building healthy relationships is to create safety within yourself.

When you feel safe in your body, you can then extend this sense of security to your relationships with others. Safety is the key to unlocking loving, connected, and fulfilling relationships. Reminding yourself that you are complete and whole, just as you are, will help to foster emotional safety from within yourself.

Exercise to Cultivate Inner Safety: Safe Space Visualization

Before we explore how to create safety within yourself, it's important to remember that this exercise is about creating emotional safety, and it should only be used after confirming that you are physically safe. Our nervous system is designed to protect us, so it's vital to honor any signals your body is sending. *If your environment feels unsafe, address that first before continuing with this practice.*

Once you've confirmed that your physical surroundings are safe, this visualization can help you create a sense of emotional security. It offers you an accessible personal retreat for those times when feelings of insecurity or fear arise.

1. Find a Quiet Place: Start by finding a comfortable, quiet space where you won't be interrupted. Sit or lie down, whichever feels best.

2. Close Your Eyes and Breathe: Gently close your eyes and take a few slow, deep breaths to relax your body. Allow your thoughts to slow down as you focus on your breathing.

3. Imagine Your Safe Space: Now, imagine yourself in a place where you feel completely safe, calm, and secure. This could be somewhere real, like a favorite spot in nature or a cozy room, or it could be an imaginary space, like a beach or a garden, where nothing can disturb you.

4. Engage Your Senses: Make this space as vivid as possible by engaging all of your senses. *What do you see—what colors or objects surround you? What can you hear—is it the sound* of waves, birds singing, or a peaceful breeze? *What do you feel*—the warmth of the sun, the softness of the ground beneath you? *What do you smell*—if you want, imagine a comforting scent in the air, like fresh flowers or the smell of rain.

5. Relax Into This Space: As you immerse yourself in your safe space, notice how your body begins to feel more at ease. Let any tension melt away, knowing that in this space, nothing can harm you. You are protected here. Stay in this visualization as long as you need, allowing yourself to feel grounded and secure.

6. Come Back Gently: When you feel ready, take a few deep breaths and slowly bring your awareness back to the present moment. Open your eyes, knowing that you can return to your safe space whenever you need emotional support or a moment of calm.

By practicing this Safe Space Visualization, you can cultivate a sense of emotional security and stability, especially in moments when your mind feels overwhelmed or anxious. Remember, this exercise is not about dismissing your emotions but about offering yourself a supportive and secure place to process them.

Another way to cultivate this inner safety is to practice mindfulness. The practice of mindfulness involves focusing on what you're experiencing in the moment, without adding your own judgments or stories. This can involve taking deep breaths, doing a body scan to check for tension or discomfort, and focusing on the sensations in our bodies. It can also just mean increased awareness of the task we are doing. By staying present, we can learn to recognize and respond to our emotions in a healthier way, rather than simply reacting out of fear or anxiety.

An important way to create safety is by establishing healthy boundaries. We will explore this topic in depth in Chapter 35, but for now it is important to note that boundaries are not solely intended to keep people out. Done right, boundaries are invitations into deeper connection.

Not only will the skills you will learn in this book help you to create a more meaningful connection in your intimate relationships, but they will also help you to foster healthy relationships with both people and experiences alike. For example, your relationship with food, money, your business, or your body can be significantly improved through the use of practical, healthy boundaries. Boundary setting can include setting limits on our time, energy, and resources to ensure that we are not overextending ourselves. By setting boundaries, we can create a sense of safety and control over our lives, which can help us feel more empowered and confident in our relationships. More on this later!

Being intentional about our recovery from stressful or traumatic events is also crucial to creating safety within ourselves. As Gabor Maté, MD so beautifully states, *"The essence of trauma is disconnection from ourselves. Trauma is not terrible things that happen from the other side—those are traumatic. But the trauma is that very separation from the body and emotions."*

These experiences may have left us forever changed, but they do not need to affect our sense of safety indefinitely. Remember, no matter what happened in the past, **you are not broken, and you don't need to be "fixed."** When we approach trauma recovery from a perspective of wholeness, we foster a loving and compassionate environment for our growth and development. Our commitment to processing and recovering from challenging events, along with gathering the tools required to navigate future challenges can help us to create, for ourselves, the safety we need so that we can get unstuck.

The autonomic nervous system, which includes the sympathetic and parasympathetic nervous systems, plays a key role in our ability to recover from stress and trauma. When we experience stress or trauma, our sympathetic nervous system goes into overdrive, triggering the fight or flight response. *In order to recover from these events, we need to activate our parasympathetic nervous system, which helps us relax and recover.*

Practical ways to activate the parasympathetic nervous system include deep breathing exercises, yoga, meditation, and spending time in nature. It is also important to engage in self-care activities, such as taking a warm bath, getting a massage, or practicing gentle movement such as walking or stretching. By taking care of ourselves in these ways, we can recover from stress and trauma more fully and create a sense of safety within our own bodies.

Creating safety is essential for establishing healthy relationships and feeling empowered in our lives. As you shift out of autopilot mode and begin to consciously create your experiences, your self trust will grow, and your confidence to communicate and connect with others will skyrocket. Recovering from stress and trauma is crucial to closing the loop and recovering the nervous system, so we can live more fully and authentically. By practicing mindfulness, setting healthy boundaries, and engaging in self-care activities, you can create a sense of safety within yourself and break free from the patterns that are keeping you stuck.

CHAPTER TWELVE

A Journey to Self-Love and Acceptance

Do you ever feel like you're not good enough for your relationship? That you're constantly falling short of the expectations placed on you? It's okay, friend. Again, you are not alone. This is a common reason so many people feel stuck in their relationships—they struggle with accepting themselves as they are. But here's the thing: **radical self-love and acceptance are the fastest ways to experience your highest and best life, and these are gifts that we must first give to ourselves.**

What does this mean, exactly?

This means *accepting things as they are while continuing to work towards your ideal experience.* You do not need to be perfectly content with the way things are to simply accept that this is in fact where you are right now. It means giving yourself the love and compassion you deserve, even if you don't feel like you've earned it. It means recognizing that you are responsible for creating the experiences you have in your life, even when it appears as though you do not. By accepting where you are right now on your journey with love and compassion, you will experience growth with so much more speed and ease than continuing to beat yourself up. *I promise.* Besides, we're all a work in progress during this lifetime. As long as you're intentionally working towards the change you desire, you are exactly where you are meant to be!

You and you alone are responsible for creating the experiences that you have in your life. And while you may not be able to control the external circumstances around you, *you always get to choose who you will be in response.* The more you love and accept yourself as a whole-ass human, flaws and all, the better you will be at extending that very same unconditional love and compassion to others. And when you can do this, you will soon be able to surrender to *what is,* and peacefully ride the waves of life while creating your own experience.

Consider the story of Jill, who spent years feeling inadequate in her relationship. Despite being a loving partner, she often felt like she fell short of her boyfriend's expectations. This led her to criticize herself harshly, often spiraling into feelings of unworthiness. After some introspection and some firm nudges from her coach—ahem, that's me!—Jill realized that her lack of self-love was impacting not only her well-being but also her relationship.

With support, she started practicing self-compassion, reminding herself that it was okay to be imperfect. Gradually, she found the strength to communicate her feelings to her boyfriend, sharing her journey towards self-acceptance. This openness transformed their dynamic, fostering a deeper emotional connection as they both began to embrace vulnerability and authenticity. Jill's journey of self-love ultimately empowered her to cultivate a healthier, more fulfilling relationship.

> **Go Deeper**
>
> As you begin this journey of self-love and acceptance, journaling can be a powerful tool for uncovering your truths. That's why I've created a special set of relationship-focused journal prompts for you (available at loveunstuck.com). We'll reference these prompts throughout our journey together, so grab them now and let's dive in!

Creating happiness is always possible... *even in the mundane moments of the daily routine.* As we humans are complex beings, we are not limited to experiencing only one emotion at a time. As you continue to practice your skills as a conscious creator you will even begin finding joy and happiness in your struggles as you begin to see challenges as opportunities for growth, and failures as feedback. You may notice that over time, you can be happy about one aspect of your experience while simultaneously being disappointed in another. For example, you may be both happy that your husband surprised you by picking up dinner on his way home, *and* disappointed that he didn't ask first since you had already made plans for the meal. There are so many opportunities for us to expand our experience by embracing the *both/and*, many of which allow for the happiness we desire.

You are worthy of love and acceptance just as you are. Keep reminding yourself of that and watch as your relationships with yourself and others begin to flourish.

CHAPTER THIRTEEN

Feel to Heal

As humans, we experience a wide range of emotions, and it is essential for us to feel and express them in order to release them. However, our society often stigmatizes emotions and teaches us to ignore or suppress them. This can lead to emotional stagnation, which can affect our relationships and cause us to feel just plain *stuck*.

Feeling your emotions is not always easy, especially when you're navigating a challenging relationship and experiencing numerous uncomfortable emotions. But it is crucial to allow your emotions to move through you because emotions are *energy in motion*. When you suppress your uncomfortable emotions, not only are they likely to cause more discomfort and pain, but it might just be the reason that you're missing out on the one thing you truly desire—deeper connections with others. **To heal our emotional wounds, we must stop resisting these feelings and instead, listen to what they may have to tell us.**

So, how can you start to feel your emotions in order to heal and improve your relationships? First, acknowledge that it is a process that requires time and patience. Start by allowing yourself to feel whatever emotions come up for you, and notice where you feel them in your body. Be gentle with yourself and practice self-compassion, remembering that it's okay to feel the way you do.

Processing Your Emotions

When approaching the topic of healing, it's important to remember that you are already whole. *Healing is not about fixing what is broken or becoming someone new, but rather about returning to the innate wholeness that is already within you.* We all have the capacity to heal our emotional wounds, but all-too-often, our past repression has made it a challenge for us to access these innate skills. It is by allowing ourselves to feel our emotions and engage in inner child healing, that we can begin to release the layers of conditioning and false beliefs that have covered up our wholeness. When we reconnect with our true selves, we can access our emotions in a new way. This allows us to show up in our relationships with more authenticity and vulnerability, which can deepen our connections and bring more joy and fulfillment into our lives. **Healing is not about *becoming*; it's about *remembering* our wholeness.**

Recognizing your wholeness also means observing that you are capable of feeling all the emotions—in fact, they are in large part what makes you gloriously fucking human. Knowing that you can (and likely will!) experience all the emotions at different times in your life can help reduce your discomfort around feeling some of the most uncomfortable emotions. Knowing that these uncomfortable feelings don't make you any *less than,* but rather contribute to your magical *wholeness* can really help you to look at these emotions with a new lens. By holding space for all emotions, comfortable or not, you will improve your ability to feel and process, rather than resist and suppress.

Processing your emotions is the next step, and this can involve journaling, talking to a trusted friend or therapist, or engaging in creative outlets. As you become more comfortable with feeling and processing your emotions, you will likely notice a shift in your relationships. As you build your own greater capacity for experiencing your emotions, you also have the additional benefit of increased capacity for experiencing others' emotions. As a result of this work, you will become more empathetic and understanding towards others and feel more comfortable expressing your emotions in a healthy and constructive way, leading to deeper connections with others.

Many of us struggle to process and express our emotions because we carry wounds from our past, especially from our childhood. These wounds shape our beliefs and behaviors and yet we can often overlook them. For example, if you were told by adults that as a child that you were expected to be seen and not heard, you may have responded by making yourself small and quiet. As an adult, you may be perpetuating these patterns by not expressing yourself or your needs to not "bother" others. This is where *inner child* healing comes in, which involves acknowledging all our parts, and healing the unhealed wounds and traumas of our past.

Healing Your Emotional Inner Child

To begin the process of inner child healing, create a safe and loving space for yourself (see the exercise in Chapter 11). You may wish to incorporate a daily self-care routine, such as meditation or journaling, to more deeply connect with your inner child and start building a nurturing relationship with them. Revisiting childhood memories and allowing yourself to feel the emotions that come up can also be helpful, though it is important not to spend so much time reliving your past story that you become re-traumatized. This process can be difficult and painful, but it is crucial for healing and releasing negative emotions.

Inner child healing not only helps you process and express your emotions more effectively but also has a positive impact on your relationships. By nurturing and caring for your inner child (this is also *you!*), you will be better equipped to nurture and care for your relationships. You will communicate more effectively and empathetically, and you will be more open to giving and receiving love.

By committing to the processes of feeling to heal and returning to your wholeness, you will be taking an important step towards living a happier, healthier, and more fulfilling life, both for yourself and your relationships.

Unmask Yourself

As we've explored the benefits of healing our emotions and inner child, you may have realized how much of yourself you've been hiding. It's exhausting pretending to be someone you're not just to fit in and be accepted, isn't it? Many of us have been conditioned by society, family, and friends to contort ourselves into someone else's idea of perfection.

But here's the thing: **This self-preserving safety net of wearing masks (keeping those less desirable parts of you hidden away) actually prevents you from experiencing the fullness of what relationships can truly offer.** The only way to deeply connect with yourself and others is by embracing your authentic self. It's time to take off the masks and show up as you are.

And let me be clear, this isn't about being perfect or always "having it together," because that simply isn't realistic. Rather, it's about being fully fucking expressed in your truth and allowing others to see and love the real you. *The whole you.* Being authentic means being genuine, vulnerable, and unapologetically yourself in your relationships.

One thing I've observed time and time again is that the more authentically I live, the more I attract people who really, truly appreciate the real me. The more *me* that I am, the more I connect with people who make relationships feel safe, easy and full of love.

Things shift quickly once you learn how to embrace your personal truths, gifts, and yes, even your perceived "weaknesses" unapologetically, because it is from this space of complete self-acceptance that we become empowered to create the experiences we most desire.

So how do you become fully and authentically expressed? It starts with connecting inwardly with yourself. Take some time to get to know yourself on a deeper level. Ask yourself what your values are, what makes you feel alive, and what brings you joy. Consider your beliefs and mindsets and take inventory of the personal reality you've been creating. When you're in touch with these things, it's easier to show up as your true self because you'll have a much greater clarity around both where you're starting out and where you're hoping to go. You will soon begin to realize that even your "imperfections" are in fact perfectly ordained for you and your unique human experience.

In order to be the limitless being that you are, you must release the programming and conditioning that has kept you safe and small. It's time to let go of the beliefs that you have to hustle to measure up, that you have to be perfect to be worthy, or that you have to fit in to be accepted. These limiting beliefs only serve to keep you small—and they prevent you from living your best life.

Becoming authentically yourself is a journey, not a destination. It won't happen overnight, and it may not always be easy. But the reward of living a life true to yourself is worth it. When you're authentic, some people may fall away but you will always end up attracting the people (*your people!*) and experiences that align with who you truly are. Besides, it is much better to experience a sense of belonging than a sense of merely fitting in.

So, take a deep breath and unmask yourself. Show up as you are and start to allow others to see the real you. And remember, you're not alone on this journey. We're all in this together, doing the best we can.

Ready for a journey of self-discovery so that you can finally build the confidence and self-love required to unmask? My *Unstuck for Women Daily Self Discovery Journal* is an incredible tool for embarking on this very journey of compassionate self-inquiry and creating intentional space for growth. If you're ready to deepen the connection you have with yourself and attain greater clarity over your direction and desires, I encourage you to check it out!

CHAPTER FOURTEEN

Trusting Your Intuition

YOU KNOW THOSE TIMES when you meet someone new and instantly have a "gut feeling" about them? That's your intuition speaking. Trusting your intuition is like having a reliable inner compass that guides you through life. It's a powerful tool that can help you navigate challenging situations, make better decisions, and ultimately, lead a more fulfilling life. **Unfortunately, many people have learned to distrust or ignore their inner wisdom, often overriding it with excessive logic, stories, judgments, and old limiting programming.**

Have you ever met someone and had an initial impression of them that made you step back and keep your distance, only to later discover that you completely dodged a bullet by not engaging with them? I remember a time when I met a parent at school who on the surface seemed very kind and friendly, yet somehow "gave me the ick." I couldn't explain it, but something felt "off" to me about them, so I politely declined their invitation to get the kids together for a playdate. Not more than a couple of years later, I learned this person had been arrested for some disturbing behaviors involving children that I won't further detail here. To say I was glad I had listened to my intuition would be an understatement. My intuition in this case may have indeed protected both me and my son from harm.

If you're struggling in your relationships, learning to trust your intuition can be an absolute game-changer. Being in touch with your intuition can help you see situations from a fresh new perspective and find creative solutions that you might not have considered otherwise.

Learning to Trust Yourself

So how do you hear your intuition and develop more self-trust? It can be easier than you'd expect. Our thoughts and beliefs can create a lot of static making it really hard to hear our inner wisdom. *The first step is to quiet the noise in your mind.* If your mind is anything like mine, it's often cluttered with mentally adding to the grocery list, trying to sort out how you'll make dinner *and* get the kids to their practice on time, not to mention trying to remember *why the hell I came into this room.* Taking some time to meditate, journal, or simply be still and quiet will help you tune in to your intuition and distinguish it from the other noise in your mind.

Next, pay attention to your body. Your emotions are your inner barometer, and they are there to help you navigate your human experience. Our bodies give us signals when something is off, but far too often, we've learned to ignore them. For example, when you wake up with an upset stomach but there is no physical cause for it, you might consider other reasons you might be unsettled (for example, anxiety about an upcoming decision you must make).

Notice how your body physically reacts in various situations, starting to observe how your body is communicating with you. Do you feel tension in your stomach when you are in a disagreement with your partner? A tightness in your chest when you consider how long your to-do list is? Butterflies in your stomach when you are about to bring up a difficult topic? Or a sense of calm and peace throughout your being when you enjoy your quiet morning coffee before everyone else wakes up? These physical cues will give you invaluable information about what your intuition is trying to tell you—it's up to you to listen.

Ready to level up your intuition and tap into your inner wisdom when it comes to making decisions? Here's one way you can start to *hear* what your intuition is telling you, so that you can start building self-trust, one decision at a time.

Exercise to Hear Your Intuition: The Lean Test

One simple way to tap into your intuition is through the Lean Test. Here's how it works:

1. Stand up straight with your feet shoulder-width apart and your weight evenly distributed.

2. Ask yourself a clear, simple yes or no question; for example, "Is this purchase right for me?"

3. As you ask the question, allow your body to sway. If your body naturally leans forward, this is a "yes" from your intuition. If you naturally lean backward, this indicates a "no."

4. Take a moment to observe how your body responds, trusting this physical feedback as a reflection of your inner wisdom.

Once you've learned to hear your intuition, it's important not to override it with excessive logic, stories, judgments, and old limiting programming. This is where The Spiral Stopper Method, from my book, *Unstuck for Women*, comes in handy. Instead of storytelling or trying to understand the meaning behind your emotions, you'll want to take swift, aligned action based on what your intuition is telling you. *This means following through on the insights you receive, even when they don't make sense logically.*

I realize this isn't always easy, however consistently taking action based on your intuition will help you build the self-trust that is essential for creating healthy relationships. **When you trust yourself, you're more likely to make decisions that align with your values and needs, even if they're not popular or easy.** Doing so will help you communicate more authentically, set healthy boundaries, and ultimately, create more fulfilling relationships across the board.

So go ahead... trust your inner wisdom and watch your relationships flourish. Besides, if you can't trust yourself, who *can* you trust?

CHAPTER FIFTEEN

Building Emotional Intelligence (EQ)

EMOTIONAL INTELLIGENCE (EQ) IS the ability to recognize and understand our own emotions, as well as the emotions of others. By building our EQ, we are better equipped to hold space for others, to have greater compassion and empathy, and to better understand what's really happening when we are in conflict. **EQ plays an essential role in enhancing communication and deepening intimacy.** There are five steps towards building EQ.

How to Increase Your Emotional Intelligence (EQ)

STEP ONE: Self-awareness. Take the time to reflect on your own emotions and how they affect your behavior. By understanding your attachment style, triggers and patterns, you can begin to regulate your emotions and respond in a more intentional and productive way.

STEP TWO: Empathy. Put yourself in the shoes of others and make an effort to understand their emotions and perspective. By doing so, you can create a space for open and honest communication and work towards a mutual understanding.

STEP THREE: Active listening. Be fully present and engaged in a conversation, without judgment or distraction. By actually hearing and understanding what others are saying, you can better respond and connect with them on a deeper level.

STEP FOUR: Recognize and understand nonverbal communication. This includes body language, tone of voice, and facial expressions. By paying attention to these cues, you can better understand the emotions and intentions of others, even when they may not be explicitly stated.

STEP FIVE: Emotional regulation. Manage your own emotions in a healthy and constructive way, rather than allowing them to control your behavior. By doing so, you can create a safe and supportive environment for yourself and others, even in the midst of conflict or difficult situations.

Being present in the moment without judgment or distraction can help us develop a greater awareness of our thoughts, feelings, and behaviors. As we learn to recognize our own emotional triggers, understand our own patterns of behavior, and gain a greater sense of self-awareness, we also become more attuned to the emotions and needs of others, which can lead to greater compassion, empathy, and understanding in our relationships.

It is important to note that humans are capable of—and do!—feel a wide range of emotions on a regular basis. Remember, *you are not your emotions, and your emotions do not define you.* This means, for example, that despite feeling grumpy from time to time (or even a lot of the time), YOU are not a grump.

When experiencing emotions, *a part of you* may be feeling those emotions, but this does not mean that the emotions *are you*. Recognizing the complexity of our emotions and taking the time to understand the message being delivered by our emotions will help us to stop over-associating our identity with these fleeting physical sensations. Instead, we can begin to discover the useful information they are relaying to us.

Often, our natural autopilot response is related to our *past* unresolved emotions. We can make far better decisions when our information is based on the current reality, rather than our past. It's time to ditch the less-than-effective autopilot reaction and swap in conscious creation. You are, after all, a creator! **With practice, we can learn to observe our emotions and then consciously choose our response to them.**

As you practice choosing your response, you will see that your emotions are guides, but you are still the one deciding what to do with that guidance. By allowing our emotions to be felt (Chapter 13), we reduce the likelihood of physical and mental illness caused by suppression of emotion. The more we allow ourselves to sit in observation, the more we learn about this incredible inner guidance system. And because of better understanding and tolerating our own emotions, we become far better equipped to deal with others' emotions—whether they are difficult to deal with or not, and whether they are related to us or not. *Hello, unfuckwithable me, I've been waiting for you!*

By building your emotional intelligence, you can cultivate stronger and more fulfilling relationships, filled with empathy, understanding, and connection. It takes practice and effort, but the rewards are well worth it. Since step one of improving your EQ is self-awareness, it's important to explore those common patterns and behaviors that can cause unnecessary issues in your relationships. Let's start with one of the most significant influences on how we connect with others: our attachment style.

CHAPTER SIXTEEN

Decoding Attachment Dynamics

UNDERSTANDING ATTACHMENT STYLES AND the dynamics they create is a crucial aspect of further developing emotional intelligence. Our attachment style, formed early in life based on our experiences with caregivers, profoundly influences how we approach relationships and interact with others. There are four primary attachment styles: secure, anxious, avoidant, and disorganized. Let's break it down and take a look at how each attachment style influences both our emotional intelligence and the way we show up in relationships.

Secure Attachment

Securely attached individuals have a rock-solid foundation of self-worth and comfort with intimacy. Expressing emotions openly and creating healthy boundaries is like second nature to them. In relationships, they effortlessly empathize and respond to their partner's needs, fostering an unwavering sense of safety and trust. *Livin' the dream, amirite?*

Anxious Attachment

Anxiously attached individuals often harbor a fear of abandonment and seek constant reassurance from their partners. Sometimes, they can be hypersensitive to perceived threats, and managing their emotions might be a bit of a challenge. This heightened emotional reactivity can sometimes hinder their ability to truly understand their partner's feelings, leading to more misunderstandings.

Avoidant Attachment

Avoidant individuals tend to prioritize their independence and might find it hard to express their emotions openly. Shielding themselves from vulnerability is their M.O. and it's all done in an effort to avoid perceived rejection. This can sometimes create hurdles in relationships, as they may struggle to tune in to their partner's emotions and needs.

Disorganized Attachment

Sometimes people have a blend of both anxious and avoidant traits. Individuals with this attachment style might have experienced childhood trauma or inconsistent caregiving. They may find themselves struggling with emotional regulation, often oscillating between seeking closeness and pushing others away. It's a complex dynamic that can make understanding and expressing emotions—and as a result, relationships—a challenge.

Attached? Now, Let's Dance!

The reality is, **you can be either securely attached, or insecurely attached with a variety of coping mechanisms.** In fact, the insecure attachment categories are defined more by the individual's *coping mechanisms* than by anything else. By identifying our own attachment style and coping methods, along with those of our partners, we gain helpful insights into our emotional patterns and how we interact in relationship to others. This awareness allows us to approach conflicts and challenges with greater empathy, opening the door for greater understanding and deeper connection.

When two people with different attachment styles come together in a relationship, they can encounter some very interesting "dances." Following are some common dynamics that result from differing attachment styles to be aware of.

Common Attachment Style Dances

The Pursuer-Distancer Polka

When it comes to attachment styles, it's like a dance between a passionate pursuer and a cautious distancer. Imagine one partner with an anxious attachment style, craving closeness and reassurance, while the other partner has an avoidant style, needing space to maintain their independence. This can lead to a *push-and-pull dynamic* where the anxious partner seeks more, and the avoidant partner retreats further, leaving both feeling frustrated and emotionally distant.

The Retreat Rumba

Picture this—an avoidant partner who learned to lock away their emotions in childhood as a way to cope. Now, imagine them paired with a partner who freely expresses their feelings, a partner with a secure attachment style. The avoidant partner's *emotional shutdown* can often leave their partner feeling neglected and their own emotions unaddressed.

The Fear of Abandonment Foxtrot

Enter the anxious individuals with their intense fear of abandonment. Even the slightest signs of disconnection from their partner can set off alarm bells, causing anxiety levels to skyrocket. On the flip side, their avoidant partner might struggle to understand and meet their partner's need for reassurance, leaving them feeling *rejected and emotionally adrift.*

The Conflict Resolution Cha-Cha

Imagine an anxious partner who wants to resolve issues right away and seeks emotional validation, cha-cha-ing right up to their avoidant partner who fears conflict and emotionally withdraws to protect themselves. This mismatched dance can leave both partners feeling *unheard and frustrated.*

The Self-Sufficiency Swing

Step into the world of avoidant partners who cherish their independence and self-sufficiency. Now, imagine them twirling around the dance floor with anxious partners who crave emotional dependency and validation. These differing needs for autonomy and connection can create *tension and misunderstandings* in the relationship (unless, of course, you realize that you can have *both* autonomy *and* connection!).

The Vulnerability Tango

For this dance, picture partners with varying comfort levels when it comes to vulnerability. Anxious individuals may be more open and expressive with their emotions, while avoidant partners may struggle to share their deeper feelings. This can lead to a lack of emotional intimacy and *difficulty in truly connecting* with each other.

It's essential to recognize that while these attachment style dynamics can lead to challenges, there's hope for improvement. By nurturing emotional intelligence and practicing open and honest communication, **couples can learn to understand each other better and create a secure and supportive relationship environment.**

With empathy, active listening, and a shared commitment to personal growth, partners can master these once-tricky dance moves and navigate life's challenges together, fostering emotional intimacy and strengthening their connection.

Chapter Seventeen

Love Without Expectation

As humans, we often find ourselves in a fruitless game of scorekeeping in our relationships. We keep track of the things we do for others and expect something in return... and when they don't do as we expect, *we feel resentful and unappreciated.* This game may seem like an attempt to create "fairness," but the truth is that this approach is limiting to both you and your relationships. I mean, who wants to receive a gift that someone feels obligated to give simply to keep the score even? No thank you!

To break free from the game of scorekeeping, you need to embrace radical responsibility in your relationships, starting with the relationship you have with yourself. It's not about shame, guilt, fault, or blame; it's about taking responsibility for your actions and your role in the relationship. If you want strong and healthy relationships with others, you absolutely must shift your focus from *being right, winning, and keeping score* to repairing the damage done and starting fresh.

Love never keeps score.

At this point in my life, I simply refuse to compete or scorekeep with anyone. Life is too short to spend it comparing myself to nor competing with anyone else. And because I was only ever meant to be *me*, both comparison and competition only keep me trapped and limited.

The problem with trying to change your partner or their behavior (no matter how subtle you think you are going about it) is that this expectation of change is setting you up for certain disappointment. The harsh reality is that when you focus on the actions of others, you lose sight of your own actions. **It is far too easy to become trapped in this scorekeeping game that has no winners. This game is one where the cost of winning is the loss of connection.**

In addition, when you give with parameters and expectations, you limit your ability to receive even greater things in return. What a shame for you to miss out on all of the abundant love you could be experiencing! The real rub is, *you will receive the kind of love you give, not the kind of love you want.* If you give fearful, obligatory or performative "love," you will miss out on experiencing the full unconditional love you deserve.

Thankfully, there's another way. You can choose to give freely without expectation, by learning to love unconditionally. It's time to let go of judgment, assumptions, and expectations and to start giving freely. Though it might seem scary or difficult to give without expectation at first, I promise it will absolutely be worth it!

You can start by letting go of your stories and judgments in order to make space for new experiences. For example, when you stop complaining that your partner never does anything helpful and you start appreciating the helpful things they *do* do, you'll not only *feel better* about their contribution, but you'll likely also see them become even more helpful as a result of your gratitude and appreciation. The little things you do really can make a huge difference. It's time to take responsibility for yourself. If you desire things to be different, you've got to become aware of your actions and vulnerabilities, and work on developing the relationship you have with yourself.

Besides… **love with limits isn't truly love at all.**

When you stop giving with the expectation of receiving, and start giving freely without limits, *you* take control of your experience. The gifts you receive in return may not come from who or where you expect, or on the timeline you had hoped for, but when you've made this shift, you will experience more abundance than you can imagine.

By releasing expectations and pressure, you open yourself up to new opportunities and experiences, and when you give freely without expectation, you create space for true connection and love to flourish. Embrace radical responsibility in your relationships and watch as your love multiplies. Besides, the true purpose of relationships isn't just about what you can *get* from another person, but about what you can both co-create together.

CHAPTER EIGHTEEN

The True Purpose of Relationships

IT'S EASY TO FALL into the trap of thinking that relationships are all about what you can get from them. But what if I told you that you've been looking at relationships all wrong?

The true purpose of a relationship is not about what you can get from it, but rather what you can give to it.

Relationships are opportunities to give, learn, and grow with intention. They are spaces where we can choose to show up as our best selves and create meaningful experiences with another person. *When we focus on what we can give to our relationships, rather than what we can get from them, we open ourselves up to a world of possibilities.*

So, when you're feeling stuck in your relationship, it's the perfect time to shift your perspective. Instead of focusing on what your partner is or isn't doing, ask yourself: *How can I show up differently? How can I create a new experience for myself and my partner?* Remember, you are in control of your own experience, and the only way to create change is by acting.

Take a moment to think about what you want from your relationship. Do you want more intimacy, more support, more communication, or more fun? Whatever it is, ask yourself what you can do to *create that experience for yourself* and your partner. Maybe it's taking the initiative to plan a date night or having a difficult conversation that you've been avoiding.

Consider Jo, who struggled with feeling disconnected in their relationship. They often felt like their partner didn't understand their needs and became frustrated, focusing on the perceived shortcomings in their partner's actions. After some self-reflection, Jo realized they had been waiting for their partner to make changes instead of considering what they could bring to the relationship. Inspired to shift their perspective, Jo took intentional action by approaching their partner with an open heart. They expressed their desire for a more meaningful connection, outlining what that could look like.

In this process, Jo embraced the idea of both giving and growing. By openly sharing their needs, they created space for their partner to do the same. Their honest dialogue helped them both acknowledge each other's imperfections while reinforcing their commitment to acceptance. Jo learned that by focusing on what they could give—vulnerability, communication, and love—they could co-create a more fulfilling relationship. This journey of giving and growing exemplifies how shifting our focus can lead to transformative change in our relationships.

In the end, the true goal of a relationship is not about finding someone who "completes you." That is a myth perpetuated by pop culture.

The real goal of relationship is to find someone who completely accepts you. It's about being intentional with your actions, showing up as the best version of yourself, and creating a space where you can grow together.

You have the power to create the relationship of your dreams, so get out there and take action to make it happen.

CHAPTER NINETEEN

Balancing Energy and Creating Space

YOU MAY HAVE HEARD the saying, "relationships are a two-way street," but have you ever stopped to think about what that really means? It means that *both partners need to be equally invested in and committed to creating a healthy and fulfilling relationship.* As I mentioned earlier, it's not just about what you can get from your partner, but also what you can give to them.

Think of your relationship as a recipe where you need the right "ingredients" to make it work. Each partner brings something unique to the mix, and it's up to both of you to contribute your best selves to create a delicious harmony. It's not about being perfect or "good enough", but rather about doing your best and being your whole self. It's not about division, it's about collaboration. It's not about receiving and dividing things up, it's about giving and what we can contribute.

When it comes to balancing energy in your relationship, it's important to recognize that each partner has different needs and priorities. You may have different schedules, workloads, and responsibilities, but that doesn't mean you can't make time for each other. However, you must be intentional about creating space for your relationship and be willing to give 100% of what you can.

Relationships are not static; they're dynamic. Setting the table for a healthy connection means showing up to the best of your abilities at any given time. It's not about keeping score or about who's giving more, but rather about both partners being fully present and engaged in the relationship. This means being willing to listen, communicate openly, and be supportive of each other.

Balancing energy in your relationship requires both partners to give 100 percent of what they can while allowing grace for any shortfalls. This doesn't look the same every day, because as humans we live in a state of perpetual change. No one is perfect, and we all have our "off" days. If either you or your partner falls short of your expectations, it's important to be understanding and forgiving.

Of course, *this doesn't mean you should tolerate toxic or unhealthy behavior,* but rather that you should approach any challenges or conflicts with compassion and empathy, both for yourself and for others.

Exercise for Balancing Your Energy: Personal Prioritization

To cultivate balance in your life and relationship, it's essential to prioritize what truly matters to you. Here's a simple exercise to help you clarify your priorities:

1. Set Aside Time: Find a quiet space where you can reflect without distractions. Allocate about 15-20 minutes for this exercise.

2. List Your Priorities: Take a moment to write down **the top five priorities** in your life right now. These could include aspects like work, family, health, personal growth, relationships, hobbies, or self-care.

3. Rank Your Priorities: Once you have your list, rank them from 1 to 5, with 1 being the most important and 5 being the least important. Consider what you feel deserves your time and energy the most.

4. Reflect: For each priority, jot down a few sentences about why it matters to you. Ask yourself:

- How does this priority contribute to my overall happiness?

- What specific actions can I take to support this priority in my life?

5. Create Action Steps: Choose **one priority** from your list to focus on this week. Write down one specific action you can take to honor that priority (e.g., scheduling time for self-care, having a meaningful conversation with a loved one, etc.).

6. Check-In: At the end of the week, reflect on how prioritizing this area has impacted your well-being and your relationships. Did you feel more balanced? Did you notice any shifts in your energy or connections?

Remember to set the table for a healthy connection by being fully present and engaged in the relationship and by staying curious. By doing so, you create the space for each other to grow and thrive and build a strong foundation for a fulfilling and stable relationship.

Next, let's explore how to overcome some common interpersonal patterns that can wreak havoc on your relationships—people pleasing, codependency, and hyper independence—so that you can reclaim your power and free yourself to create the love you want.

CHAPTER TWENTY

Ditch the People Pleasing Tendencies

IF YOU'RE LIKE ME, you've probably spent a lot of your life contorting yourself in an attempt to please others. Or maybe you find yourself agreeing to things you don't want to do or going along with others' ideas, just to avoid conflict or heightened emotions. If so, you're far from alone. Many people struggle with people pleasing tendencies, and it can leave one feeling overwhelmed, resentful, and disconnected from their true selves. *Luckily, unconditional love and acceptance always start within and will never ever require you to abandon yourself.*

Where Does People Pleasing Come From?

From a young age, many of us were raised to be the "good girl" or "good boy," taught that being obedient, polite, and agreeable were virtues to uphold. We may have even learned that these were necessary behaviors if we desired to earn favor or love from those around us. While these qualities can be important in certain contexts, they become problematic when they result in us abandoning our own needs and desires.

As children, most of us learned that behaving in ways that pleased our caregivers often resulted in rewards, praise, or at the very least, a lack of punishment. This positive reinforcement encouraged us to continue prioritizing the happiness and approval of others over our own.

For some, people pleasing even became a survival tool, used to navigate a world where we longed to fit in, avoid conflict, or gain acceptance and love. When we behaved in ways that were agreeable and accommodating, we received positive attention and avoided unpleasant consequences, solidifying the patterns.

In reality, **people pleasing is not just about being nice; it's about seeking external validation and acceptance**. We often fall into the trap of believing that by making others happy, we will secure love, acceptance, and belonging. However, this belief can lead to a never-ending cycle of seeking validation from others, leaving us drained and unfulfilled.

Ironically, the more we strive to please everyone around us, the more exhausted and unfulfilled we become. We crave love, acceptance, and belonging, but often end up feeling disappointed and resentful. Our attempts to please others don't always yield the desired results, leaving us feeling unvalidated and undervalued.

Understanding the roots of people pleasing is the first step toward breaking free from this cycle. It's essential to recognize that while this behavior may have served a useful purpose in the past, it may no longer be beneficial in our adult lives. Next, let's explore how to shift from people pleasing to authentic living, where your happiness and self-acceptance take center stage.

Breaking Free from People Pleasing

It's time to discover your authentic self and learn to live a life that feels true to who you are. It's not just about learning to say no; it's about understanding and embracing your unique identity and honoring it in every aspect of your life. Here are three tips to help you ditch those people pleasing tendencies and find lasting freedom:

Tip 1: The importance of self-awareness

One of the first steps towards rediscovering your whole authentic self is to become more self-aware. It is crucial to take the time to understand your values, beliefs, and desires, so that you can make choices that actually align with your authentic self (and not just to appease others or avoid conflict).

You can get started by asking yourself some questions: What do I really want? Like, what do I *really fucking want?* What are my values? What brings me joy? What am I passionate about?

Take the time to journal, meditate, or simply sit quietly and reflect on these questions. The more you understand yourself, the easier it will be to make choices that feel authentic and aligned with your true self. The more you shift your focus from finding what you believe is missing or broken, to observing your wholeness in its majestic glory, the more freedom you will discover.

Tip 2: Learn to set boundaries

People pleasers often struggle with setting boundaries, which can quickly lead to feeling overwhelmed, resentful, and just plain stuck. Learning to set clear boundaries and communicating them effectively can help you take control of your life and prioritize your needs.

Start by identifying where you need to set boundaries. Is it with a certain person or situation? Is it around your time, energy, or resources? Once you've identified where you need to set boundaries, practice saying "no" or "not right now" in a clear (because clear is kind) and compassionate way. Remember, saying no doesn't make you a bad person, it just means you're prioritizing your own needs.

It is crucial to set effective boundaries to care for yourself. Besides, you're not going to be much good to anyone if you're exhausted or unhealthy as a result of not taking good care of yourself. If this is not your strong suit, not to worry—we will discuss setting boundaries further in Chapter 35.

Tip 3: Embrace vulnerability and self-acceptance

Fully expressing yourself and loving yourself require a level of vulnerability that can be scary, but it's worth it. Embracing vulnerability and self-acceptance will help you let go of the need to please others and start living a life that feels authentic and fulfilling. In doing so, it's essential to cultivate self-compassion so that you can treat yourself with the same kindness and care that you would offer to a friend. The truth is you deserve it just as much as anybody!

How do you start practicing self-compassion? When you notice yourself slipping into people pleasing tendencies, take a moment to pause, breathe, and offer yourself some kind and encouraging words. Remember, you're doing the best you can, and it's okay to make mistakes. Embrace your imperfections, let go of the need to be perfect, and start living a life that feels true to who you are. As a bonus, the more you can accept yourself, the freer you will become from suffering.

Go Deeper

If you're ready to go deeper on your journey and ditch people pleasing tendencies for good, I encourage you to check out the additional resources available at loveunstuck.com. There, you'll find links to my Authenticity Unleashed program and the People Pleaser's Path to Freedom Masterclass & eBook—both designed to help you reclaim your authentic self and live a life that truly lights your soul on fire.

Ditching your people pleasing tendencies can be a bit of a process, but it's a journey worth taking. By becoming more self-aware, setting boundaries, and embracing self-acceptance, you can rediscover your authentic self and start living a life that not only feels true to who you are but also *lights your fucking soul on fire*.

Next, let's explore the dynamic of the codependent and narcissist, another challenge that may seem extremely familiar to those with people pleasing tendencies.

CHAPTER TWENTY-ONE

Codependency & Narcissism

WHEN IT COMES TO the complexities of relationships, it's essential to address the dynamics of codependency and narcissism that may trap us in cycles of pain and confusion. If you find yourself feeling stuck or questioning your reality, it's time to recognize the red flags you might have ignored at the start of your relationship. Brushing off these signs or justifying them out of fear of being alone can lead to the erosion of your boundaries and self-worth, so taking a closer look is well warranted. I would also like to make note here that **both codependency and narcissism are coping strategies in response to trauma and should be viewed with a lens of (self-) compassion and understanding.**

Perhaps you've tried expressing your needs, only to be met with defensiveness, redirection, or even gaslighting (see Table 32-1 for definitions of these common reactions). It's a painful place to be—questioning your sanity, memories, and experiences. On the other hand, true love *feels aligned*; it's about open communication, holding each other's hearts tenderly, and collaborating as a team. Many relationships with truly narcissistic partners fail because narcissism is a personality disorder, and most narcissists are not capable of the type of accountability that being part of a couple requires. You may have shared your pain with others, only to be told that it's just typical of the hardships sustained in relationship. It is ideal to seek professional support from a trained counselor, life coach, or therapist who understands the relationship dynamics unique to relationships in which your partner has a diagnosable personality disorder.

Narcissism has truly become a buzzword as of late, and with *most people in the general populations showing signs of narcissistic behavior at times*, it becomes important not to conflate narcissistic behavior with narcissistic personality disorder (NPD, which is a diagnosis attributed to a relatively small percentage of people). However, absent an NPD diagnosis, there are still some commonly experienced "narcissistic" behavioral issues that can significantly interfere with the ability to create healthy, happy relationships. These common behaviors are the focus of this chapter.

If you feel mistreated and disrespected, remember this: you don't deserve it, no matter what. Your worth is not something you need to earn, and you should never have to "fight" for love and acceptance. Should you choose to do everything you can to save your relationship with someone exhibiting narcissistic behavior, you will need to implement—*and uphold*—healthy boundaries to make the relationship "work." As you increase your understanding of the intertwined patterns of codependency and narcissism, you will also empower yourself, uncovering the ways *you need to respond* to your relationship in order to keep yourself physically, emotionally, intellectually, and spiritually safe. Following are some tips that will help you to identify the narcissist-codependent patterns that make relationships like yours more difficult than others.

Identifying Codependency and Narcissism

Sometimes, we find ourselves ensnared in relationships that really fucking drain our spirit (been there, girlfriend). It's essential to recognize the signs of codependency and narcissism if we are to break free from their grasp.

You may identify with or recognize some or all of the following codependent behaviors and experiences:

- Feeling responsible for your partner's emotions and well-being

- Neglecting your own needs to prioritize your partner's wants

- Buying into the "you complete me" myth, expecting others to fix, heal or change you

- Struggling to set and maintain healthy boundaries

- Fearing rejection or abandonment, leading to compliance with your partner's wishes

- Losing sight of your individuality and personal interests

On the other hand, you may also identify with or recognize the following narcissistic behaviors:

- An excessive need for admiration and validation

- A lack of empathy for others' feelings and needs

- Manipulative behavior to maintain control over others

- Constantly seeking attention and admiration from others

- Inability to take responsibility for their actions or apologize sincerely

If you read those lists and see yourself or your relationships within them, know that identifying what is happening is the first step. You may have even identified some patterns from *both lists* within yourself. This is normal, since as I mentioned, many of these common behaviors associated with the term *narcissism* are actually quite common amongst humans, regardless of any NPD diagnosis. The truth is, having awareness of your *relationship patterns and behaviors* is empowering because you have the power within you to make a change. Peace, love, and hope are all within your grasp. It's time to become an active participant in your life and your relationship. The message I most needed when I was struggling with the decision of whether I would stay or leave my marriage was this: **Stop waiting for things to change externally; instead, take radical responsibility for your own growth and happiness.**

I've been where you are—feeling trapped, hopeless, and unsure if happiness would ever find me again. I had to face the reality that I had given away my power and allowed my own excuses and stories to dictate my life. Things changed when I decided I had had enough of my own victim mentality. My transformation began when I took the reins, reclaimed my power, and went *from victim to victorious.*

Embrace Your Empowered Self

You are only powerless if you relinquish your power. You have the strength to set boundaries, require better for yourself, and express your needs and desires. Embrace the fact that you deserve peace, happiness, and a love that honors your boundaries. *Love flourishes within the safety of clear boundaries, where vulnerability can thrive.*

I won't sugarcoat it—if you're in a codependent relationship, changing your situation may be challenging, and it likely won't happen overnight, but the good news is that you have more control than you may have once thought. Although sometimes this involves the difficult decision to end a relationship, you are worthy of being treated well and of having the life and love that make you truly happy.

Verbal and emotional abuse are forms of abuse, and it's crucial to acknowledge that. And... *Your well-being* is *your responsibility.* You have the power to create the life you desire, and gloriously, you don't need to rely on anyone else to change it for you—not even your spouse. You alone hold the key to your happiness.

The crucial first step to healing these patterns is to focus on yourself and the way you perceive your own worth. You deserve better, and it starts with treating yourself with the love and respect you crave.

By setting boundaries and standing up for yourself, you create a safe space for love to thrive. Love is not about sacrificing your happiness; it's about mutual growth and support. Boundaries provide the space for vulnerability to flourish, fostering deeper connections that honor and respect each other's needs. We will explore the creation of healthy boundaries, along with other strategies that will help you to combat codependent tendencies in Part 3.

Embrace Empowered Intimacy

You are worthy of love, joy, and fulfillment. So, seize the reins, reclaim your power, and embrace the magnificent, imperfect, and extraordinary human experience. You have the potential to write some new beautiful chapters in your love story—ones that celebrate the love you've cultivated and the person you've become. *This is your time to shine.*

The road ahead may have its challenges, but you hold the strength within you to create a love that defies limits and a connection that stands the test of time.

Go Deeper

As this section of the book only scratches the surface of what are quite complex dynamics, I invite you to consider further exploring these patterns if they are appearing in any way in your life. The following resources, both written by experts in their field, provide greater depth and understanding on the complex topic of dealing with the codependent/narcissist dynamic as well as more in-depth strategies to help you find freedom from these challenging patterns once and for all.

Behary, Wendy T. *Disarming the Narcissist: Surviving and Thriving with the Self-Absorbed*. 3rd ed. Oakland, CA: New Harbinger Publications, 2021.

Durvasula, Ramani S. *It's Not You, It's Them: A Guide to Understanding the Narcissist in Your Life*. California: Post Hill Press, 2019.

CHAPTER TWENTY-TWO

Balancing Independence & Interdependence

IN OUR MODERN WORLD there is a real push towards self-sufficiency and the "I don't need anyone else" mentality. In fact, it's become so common to focus on this self-sufficiency that we often overlook the ancient wisdom that says it takes a village. What if we could shift our focus from independence—or hyper independence—to *interdependence*? From doing it alone to doing it together?

The Myth of Independence

Hyper independence often stems from past trauma and/or societal conditioning. Let's take a look at how these two can influence our perspective of independence and may contribute to the overly independent tendencies that can wreak havoc on our modern-day relationships.

Society has impressed the idea of being self-sufficient upon us from an early age, encouraging us to look out for #1. **In a world encouraging us to protect ourselves, provide for ourselves, and to avoid the burden of asking others for support, it is no wonder that so many struggle to loosen the reins when it comes to**

being supported within a relationship. It goes against everything we've been taught. It goes against what we believe is *necessary to survive.*

Along with this societal expectation of self-sufficiency, most of us have experienced some form of heartbreak in our lives, which may have led to the guarding of our hearts against any potential similar pain. Heartbreak is a physical, emotional, and psychological experience, and understanding this can help navigate our intense emotions. As I've experienced in my own journey through two divorces and one broken engagement, *self-abandonment often stems from a deep-seated fear of being abandoned.* In response to our fear of abandonment, whether consciously or not, we can often end up contorting ourselves, hoping to be loved and, at the very least, avoiding the risk of further abandonment and pain.

But what we often don't realize is that in doing so, we abandon the one person who's always been there for us: *ourselves.* It took me going through some pretty difficult times to see that the whole time I was trying to protect my heart by holding on so tight, I was actually leaving myself behind. Oh, the irony.

By guarding our hearts against future heartbreak, we actively prevent ourselves from experiencing the future love we desire the most. This adventure into new love does require a leap of faith and a risk of heartbreak, *but it is absolutely fucking worth it.* In fact, taking a chance on love is absolutely *necessary* if you desire to experience a healthy, happy relationship. *You simply cannot avoid the risk without also simultaneously avoiding the desired outcome!*

Embracing Self-Love and Vulnerability

Embracing self-love was a game-changer for me. It was the realization that we don't actually have to be less than we are in order to be loved and accepted, but rather we actually need to be fully ourselves.

Self-love means setting boundaries, recognizing our worth, and understanding that we are complete and whole all on our own.

Remember, asking for support isn't about being weak or needy. It's actually about recognizing your humanity and inviting your partner to be part of your journey. True strength lies not in our ability to do everything alone, but in our willingness to be vulnerable and open to support. As I often say, **true strength lies in your willingness to be vulnerable.**

Instead of striving for complete independence, what if we could shift our focus to interdependence? This means moving from a *power-over* approach to a *power-with* approach, where we come together and rely on the strength of our community.

This shift from a *power-over* approach to a *power-with* approach essentially eliminates the illusory hierarchy of humanity—the illusion that there are people above and below, all separate from us. This illusion and its implications truly don't serve us—we are not broken or less than, we are whole, both individually *and* as a collective. This unity perspective actually allows us to embrace expansion and evolution in a new way, based on a foundation of unconditional love and acceptance—recognition of our wholeness—rather than based on rules, conditions, and expectations that were themselves built on fear, lack, division, and separateness.

Balancing Giving and Receiving

In our relationships, it's crucial to find a balance between giving and receiving. Many of us, especially those prone to people pleasing, tend to focus solely on giving, believing that this is the key to maintaining our relationships. However, this approach can lead to burnout and resentment.

Instead, we need to cultivate spaces where we receive as much as we give. This balance allows us to contribute to our relationships without depleting ourselves, as well as receive with grace and gratitude. **In giving, not only do we help others, we also simultaneously *receive* the enriching experiences that we most long for.**

The belief that love requires us to sacrifice is a myth that many of us have lived by. But here's the truth: *sacrificing our needs leads to self-abandonment.* This can affect all relationships and can be particularly problematic when it comes to parenting. For example, trying to give your kids everything, while seemingly applauded by society, often comes at the cost of your own well-being and connection as a parent. The truth is our kids need us to show up in *our wholeness* so that they also feel safe to show up as *their whole self.* **Our kids do not need a perfect parent, they need a present one.**

Despite our expectation, sacrificing our own needs doesn't actually enrich our relationships. In fact, it often depletes them. It's crucial to find a way that allows us to be both present and connected in our relationships—without losing ourselves.

True love is about finding solutions where everyone's needs are met, and I personally believe that creating win-win solutions is nearly always possible. However, coming up with fresh ideas requires creativity, open communication, and a willingness to see beyond your own often limited perspective. It requires you to consider how *both parties* (or all parties involved) might feel fulfilled, rather than deciding which one of you gets their way. It places both parties on the same team working together, rather than pitting one against another in a competition where ultimately no one wins.

> **Exercise for Balancing Independence and Inter-dependence: Creating Win-Win Solutions**
>
> 1. Reflect on areas where you might be overextending in the name of love or self-sufficiency.
>
> 2. Practice asking for help in small ways, even if it feels uncomfortable at first.
>
> 3. Communicate openly with your loved ones about your needs and invite them to do the same.
>
> 4. Look for creative solutions that meet everyone's needs, rather than defaulting to compromise or sacrifice.
>
> 5. Cultivate self-love and self-care practices to ensure you're giving from a place of abundance.

Remember, true love supports growth and fulfillment. **If you're giving from a place of abundance and overflow, there will always be enough.** By balancing independence with interdependence and being cognizant of where you may be sacrificing too much, you can create genuine, loving connections that truly enrich your life and the lives of those around you.

CHAPTER TWENTY-THREE

Should I Stay or Should I Go?

STAYING IN AN UNHAPPY relationship because it's the "right" thing to do? I hear you, my friend. You're not alone. Many people find themselves in this situation, feeling stuck and unsure of what to do next. But before you make any decisions, let's take a closer look at what might be keeping you in a relationship that isn't really working.

First, let's explore some of the common beliefs around divorce that might be holding you back.

Are you hanging onto the idea of "till death do us part" even though it feels more like a life sentence than a sacred vow?

It's important to remember that marriage is a legal contract, not a prison sentence. While it's true that divorce can be difficult and painful, it's not a failure or a sin (I largely blame religion for this misguided and shame-causing belief, but that's a topic for a whole different book). It's simply a choice to end a relationship that is no longer serving you.

Are you fearful of disappointing other people or causing your partner more pain, all the while feeling disappointed in yourself?

It's natural to want to avoid conflict and keep the peace, but often, that comes at a cost to our own happiness and well-being. Remember that you are responsible for your own happiness, and you deserve to be with someone who loves and respects you. Period.

Are you worried about being judged for appearing as though you've "failed" or "given up," so you just keep trying to fix things?

Society has placed a lot of pressure on us to succeed in all areas of our lives, including our relationships. But the truth is, not all relationships work out, and that's okay. It doesn't mean you've failed, and it doesn't mean you're giving up. It simply means that you're choosing to prioritize your own happiness and well-being. For many, relationship success can look like *walking away from relationships that are not working.*

Are you staying "for the kids" to protect them from experiencing a "broken home?" First of all, I'd like to point out that two happy, functioning people parenting separately are far less "broken" than a family in which conflict and pain are the key themes. Secondly, while we may believe we are shielding our kids from pain by staying, we are actually increasing the likelihood that they will end up in similar painful relationships as adults, thanks to our modeling. Most of the time, that very thought is quite sobering. I know that for me personally, this realization opened my eyes to see that I was not in fact protecting them at all by staying in a relationship that I would not want them emulating. I had to *show them* what a healthy, happy relationship looks like.

Note: If you're struggling with this decision as a mother, I understand deeply how challenging this can be. I've written a special message just for mamas facing this crossroads—you'll find it in the appendix. It shares a little more about my personal journey and the key realizations that helped me find clarity in this difficult decision.

It's also worth noting that **many of the "rules of relationship" we've been taught are rooted in patriarchal beliefs and systems of control.** These rules were mainly created by men and maintaining their dominance was the main purpose. Guilt and shame were (and continue to be) used heavily in many religious circles to keep people "in line" and doing what they are taught is "right." But the truth is, *hell is something we often create right here on earth.*

From the time we are little, we are taught to follow the rules, listen to "authority," and behave in certain ways. Much of society's systems are built on these undercurrents of controlled behavior—so much so that we may be completely unaware of the impacts of these systems in our daily lives and our ability to create the life we desire.

But here's the thing: *no one should stay in a relationship that is making them miserable*, and it's not just women that this applies to. You do not have to continue suffering or be a martyr to make others happy. This is simply a pattern, and you can break free of it. A lot of clarity can come from asking yourself: *Is this relationship truly out of alignment for me* or am I simply avoiding putting in the work by seeking something I think will be better?

Relationships do require effort, but they shouldn't be a constant struggle. There's a difference between putting in the work to grow together and struggling and facing nonstop challenges.

Facing the stay or go decision is a monumental moment in most of our lives, challenging us to listen closely to our inner wisdom and to identify what truly resonates with our spirit. Yes, you *can* put yourself and your needs first—and it's not selfish to do so, despite what you've been told your entire life about being a "good girl" and taking care of others above your own needs. You *can* end a marriage that is not for your highest good, despite what you've been conditioned to believe about divorce being "wrong" or "bad." And you *can* reprogram the beliefs and mindsets that have been keeping you stuck. **You can change your brain, your life, your whole world. You are that powerful, and you are that worthy of love.**

If you're feeling unsure about what to do next, I encourage you to seek support from a trusted friend, family member, or therapist. You don't have to go through this alone. The time to create your happy relationship is now, and yes—you deserve it.

"Love yourself so much that when someone treats you wrong, you recognize it."

Rena Rose

CHAPTER TWENTY-FOUR

Reclaim Your Power

I UNDERSTAND HOW IT feels to be stuck in a relationship, feeling powerless and hopeless to make a change. But I want to remind you that you cannot actually be powerless unless you choose to be. For example, peace, love, and hope were always within me, but in my past, I have at times been merely a passive participant, waiting for circumstances or other people to change. This passivity effectively rendered me both powerless and hopeless, trapping me in a life constructed from my excuses and stories. *Peace, love, and hope have always been within you, too. Even if you aren't currently experiencing them. Even if you don't remember ever having experienced them.*

It's crucial to recognize that when we're stuck in survival mode, our brain's primary focus is self-preservation. In this state, we're unable to see beyond our immediate fears and concerns. When we don't feel safe, we often miss the choices before us and typically respond in favor of maintaining the status quo, rather than from a position of power. **The safety we've created within ourselves thus becomes the foundation for reclaiming our power.**

It wasn't until I decided that I had enough of my own excuses and stories that my circumstances changed. Things around me changed because *I changed and the way I saw things changed.* I had only felt so powerless in my life because I had relinquished my power. With deeper self-awareness, I have been able to navigate my life and relationships with more clarity and confidence, fostering connections that fully honor both me and my loved ones.

Once we're out of survival mode, we can see our relationships more holistically. We can recognize that our partner's actions or words, which might have seemed threatening or hurtful when we were in survival mode, may come from a place of their own fears or needs. This understanding doesn't excuse harmful behavior, but it does allow us to respond more effectively and compassionately.

Your power cannot be taken from you, and you cannot give it away. However, you can *believe yourself to be powerless*. The good news is that you can reclaim your power and change your life at any time, you simply have to decide to. You don't need to rely on anyone else to change in order to have the peace and happiness you desire—again, you alone hold the key to your happiness! **The love you desire is actually within you, not someone else. What you need is not a partner to love you, but to first learn to love yourself.**

Ready to reclaim your power? *It all starts with you.* Start by taking radical responsibility for yourself. Stop listening to and accepting your excuses and stories. They will only keep you trapped in a life that you're not in love with. Likewise, stop waiting for other people to validate you, change for you, love you, or create the dream life you desire (and the one you are oh-so-fucking-worthy of). This waiting around is *not* you standing in your power.

When you reclaim your power, you open up the possibility of deeper, more authentic connections. You create space not just for your own growth, but for the growth of your relationships as well. As you shift out of autopilot mode and begin to consciously create your experiences, your self-trust will grow, and your confidence to communicate and connect with others will naturally expand.

Some fear that standing in their power might push people away or cost them relationships. The truth? Your authentic power may indeed repel some people, but these are precisely the people who aren't aligned with your highest good. Instead, *your power becomes a beacon, naturally attracting those who resonate with your authentic self.* This magnetic effect creates the perfect foundation for building the loving relationships you truly desire.

Exercise for Reclaiming Your Power: Affirmation Practice

1. Choose Your Affirmations: Start by choosing or creating a few affirmations that resonate with you. Here are some examples:

- "I am worthy of love and happiness."

- "I have the power to change my life."

- "I am responsible for my own joy."

- "I release the excuses that hold me back."

- "I'm learning how to embrace my power."

- "I'm in the process of creating the life I desire."

2. Ensure They Feel Believable: It's important to ensure that your affirmations feel believable for you. If you don't quite feel there yet, you can modify them by using phrases like "I'm learning how to…" or "I'm in the process of…" to make them feel more truthful. *It's not helpful to "fake it till you make it," but it absolutely will change your life if you intend to "be it till you see it."*

3. Daily Practice: Set aside a few minutes each day to repeat your affirmations. You can do this in front of a mirror, write them down in a journal, or record yourself saying them and listen to the audio on repeat. Heck, you could even repeat them while driving, doing laundry or cooking dinner.

4. Feel the Words: As you speak each affirmation, allow yourself to feel the truth of the words. Visualize what your life looks like when you fully embody these affirmations. How do you feel? How do you act? *Be it till you see it.*

5. Integrate into Your Routine: Consider integrating an affirmation practice into your morning or evening routine. Practice makes progress and consistency is key when it comes to shifting your mindset and reclaiming your power.

6. Reflect: At the end of each week, take a moment to reflect on any changes you've noticed in your mindsets, feelings, or interactions with others since starting this practice.

7. Celebrate Your Progress! *We really don't do this enough!*

By incorporating this simple yet powerful affirmation practice into your daily life, you can reclaim your power and create the life you truly desire.

When you reclaim your power, you discover that **creating love isn't about finding it outside yourself—it's about allowing what's already within you to flow outward.**

As you've moved through your journey of getting unstuck, you've built a foundation of self-awareness, learned to break free from limiting patterns, and reconnected with your authentic power.

Now you're ready for the final piece of transformation: *consciously creating the love you desire*. By combining your reclaimed power with intentional creation, you'll discover how to manifest relationships that truly reflect your inner worth.

CHAPTER TWENTY-FIVE

Create the Love

YOU MAY HAVE HEARD the saying, "What you focus on expands." This rings true in all areas of our lives, including our relationships. If you want to attract more love, joy, connection and abundance into your life, it's essential to cultivate an attitude of gratitude and mindfulness.

Gratitude

Gratitude is a powerful tool that can help you shift your focus from what's missing in your life to what's already present. By taking time to acknowledge the good in your life, you intentionally create space for more positivity to flow in.

One way to incorporate gratitude into your daily life is through implementing a gratitude practice. This could be as simple as writing down three things you're grateful for each morning or taking a few moments to reflect on what you're thankful for before going to bed. The key is to **make gratitude a habit** and to be consistent with it.

To support this journey of gratitude and self-discovery, I've created the *Unstuck for Women Daily Self Discovery Journal*. This journal combines a daily gratitude practice with intention setting and self-reflection prompts. It's designed to help you build a consistent practice of self-awareness and personal growth, complementing the ideas we're exploring in this book.

Whether you use a structured journal or create your own practice, the power lies in your consistency. Regular reflection and gratitude can be transformative tools in your personal growth journey, helping you cultivate a more positive mindset and deeper self-understanding.

Mindfulness

Mindfulness is another practice that can help you create the love you desire. When we're mindful, we're present in the moment, fully engaged in what's happening around us—even when it's merely our mundane everyday activities. This helps us to tune out unnecessary distractions and intentionally place our focus on what matters most.

Practicing mindfulness in relationship can be as simple as taking a few deep breaths before responding to a situation or person. By moving through the initial reaction phase before taking action, you will be far better able to respond with more clarity and intention than you are when you simply react out of habit or impulse.

When you combine gratitude and mindfulness, you create a powerful force that can transform your relationships and your life. **By focusing on the good things** in your life and being present in the moment, you will attract more of what you desire into your life.

Remember, creating the love you desire isn't about finding someone to complete you—you are already whole. By knowing yourself well and by living your truth, you build the foundation for relationships that are both aligned with your deepest values and wonderfully fulfilling. **It's through self-discovery and intentional unlearning that you become aware of what is actually preventing you from having the meaningful connections you desire—you!** Looking at your patterns, tendencies and unmet needs can be uncomfortable at first, but it is this very willingness that creates an opportunity for you to grow. It can be confronting to look within, yet it is through this very act of compassionate inquiry that you are able to release attachment to beliefs, mindsets and coping mechanisms that are no longer working for you. **It's as a result of cultivating the love you have within yourself that you both find freedom from unnecessary suffering *and* begin attracting relationships with people who align with your values and desires.** It's by reimagining love in a new way, that you allow love itself to transform you *from the inside out*.

As we've explored ways to get unstuck from your unhelpful patterns and beliefs, you have likely realized just how much they have been affecting your relationships. By becoming more self-aware and working on your personal growth, you have created the foundation for building the connections you truly desire. Now, it's time to take things to the next level. It's time to learn the secrets to consciously creating the healthy, loving relationships you've always longed for.

Part 3

Creating Conscious Relationships

"To fall in love with yourself is the first secret to happiness."
Robert Morley

CHAPTER TWENTY-SIX

Redefining Relationship

FORGET EVERYTHING YOU THOUGHT you knew about relationships—it's time to rewrite the rulebook and create connections that light your soul on fire!

In Parts 1 and 2, we explored key perspective shifts and strategies to get unstuck. Now, as we embark on Part 3, it's time to reimagine what relationships can truly be. Society may have led us to believe that relationships are all about what we can receive, but relationships are actually about what we can give. Relationships are not about coming together to experience obligation and discipline, and they are not a place to stick it out to prove your worth, your dedication, your perfection or your ability to be liked by others. **Relationships are about creating a space for personal growth, learning, and experience, acting as a mirror, reflecting back to us the things that we need to work on or address within ourselves.** *Relationships are the mirror through which we can observe our reflection.*

In Part 3, we'll explore powerful shifts that can transform your relationships, moving from the common challenges addressed in Part 2, to empowering solutions:

1. From Problem-Focused to Solution-Seeking: Instead of dwelling on what's wrong, you'll learn to become a proactive solution seeker, fostering growth and positive change in your relationships. (Chapter 36: Becoming a Solution Seeker)

2. From Surface-Level Chemistry to Deep Connection: Move beyond the myth that chemistry is everything, and discover how to cultivate intentional, meaningful connections that stand the test of time. (Chapter 28: Redefining Intimacy)

3. From Self-Sacrifice to Self-Care: Learn how prioritizing your own well-being actually strengthens your relationships, replacing burnout from overgiving with sustainable love and connection. (Chapter 37: Self-Care Isn't Selfish)

4. From Unspoken Expectations to Clear Communication: Develop the skills to express your needs clearly and listen actively, replacing misunderstandings with mutual understanding. (Chapter 32: Improving Communication)

5. From Conflict-Avoidance to Constructive Engagement: Discover how to navigate disagreements in a healthy way, turning potential conflicts into opportunities for deeper understanding and growth. (Chapter 34: Navigating Conflict)

6. From People Pleasing to Authentic Expression: Learn how to express your true self and set healthy boundaries, fostering deeper connections built on mutual respect and understanding. (Chapter 35: Trust & Boundaries)

7. From External Validation to Self-Trust: Develop a strong sense of self-worth and inner guidance, enhancing both your individual growth and your capacity for healthy relationships. (Chapter 38: Self-Trust)

Throughout this section, you'll gain practical tools and insights to make these empowering shifts, creating more fulfilling and conscious relationships.

These shifts represent a fundamental change in how we approach relationships. They challenge us to move beyond traditional ideas of compromise and balance, *inviting us to embrace a more dynamic and holistic view of partnership.*

To achieve this kind of personal growth and learning, we need to refine our approach to relationships. Conscious relationships are not about meeting halfway or giving half-effort. Instead, they require us to give 100 percent of what we have available at any given moment. This means giving freely and completely, without expecting anything in return. Of course, 100 percent doesn't always look the same. **Some days we have more to give than others, but it's important to always give from a place of abundance, in ways that are not to our own detriment.**

The myth that relationships should be 50/50 has been floating around for a long time. However, just because an idea has been around for a long time does *not* mean that it is correct. What I've discovered firsthand is that *not only does this 50/50 approach not work*, but it also sets us up for massive amounts of struggle and disappointment.

In conscious relationships, there is a dance between partners, each lifting up the other when they have less to give. It's important to note that each person maintains complete responsibility for their own happiness, growth, and boundaries. This means that you cannot rely on your partner to fulfill all your needs or make you happy. Instead, you must **take ownership of your own well-being and growth, while also giving your partner the space to do the same**. By embracing this mindset and redefining what we believe relationships are for, we can create truly fulfilling and transformative connections with those around us. While you're at it, give yourself grace, give your partner grace, and give those around you a little extra dose of grace and see if you can't find *the joy in the giving*.

Throughout this part of the book, we'll challenge these misconceptions and explore:

- How to redefine success in relationships

- The power of curiosity in deepening connections

- Ways to reframe limiting beliefs about love

- The importance of support and accountability

- Techniques for improving communication

- How to navigate triggers and conflict productively

- The role of trust and boundaries in healthy relationships

- Becoming a solution seeker in your partnerships

By embracing these concepts, you'll discover:

- A newfound sense of freedom and authenticity in your relationships

- The joy of giving without expectation

- A deeper understanding of yourself and your partner

- The ability to create a relationship that evolves and grows with you

In this section, we'll embark on the adventure of consciously creating relationships built on a foundation of wholeness, trust, vulnerability, connection, listening, curiosity, growth, and teamwork. We'll explore how to share a deep understanding of each other's needs, desires, and boundaries, and how to create a safe space for expressing ourselves freely, without fear of judgment or rejection.

In redefining relationships, you may realize there is now space for more possibility than you thought previously. *In what other ways might you reimagine love changing everything from the inside out?*

By the end of part 2, you'll have a fresh perspective on what relationships can be, along with practical tools to create the deep, meaningful connections you desire. You'll understand how to give yourself and others grace, find joy in giving, and open up to new possibilities in love.

Are you ready to reimagine love and change everything from the inside out? Let's dive in and discover the transformative power of conscious relationships!

CHAPTER TWENTY-SEVEN

Redefining Success

WHEN IT COMES TO redefining success in a relationship, it's important to understand that it's not about meeting a certain set of external expectations or societal norms. A successful relationship fosters a healthy harmony between togetherness and individuality, allowing both partners to grow, not just together, but as individuals too.

To do this, it's essential to first focus on the self. As mentioned before, **no one else is coming to save you**—it's crucial that you save yourself. This means taking the time to get clarity on your own values, needs, and desires, and setting intentions for what you want to create in your partnership. It means taking personal responsibility for your own experience, by practicing self-awareness and compassionate self-discovery. It means learning to *love yourself and accept yourself.*

You get what you give in a relationship. If you give conditional or performative love, you will not receive the full unconditional love that you are meant to experience. This is why it's absolutely essential that you focus on giving yourself the love and care that you need first, so that you can then give to others from your own abundance of love and care.

When both individuals in a relationship are happy and fulfilled within themselves, the relationship can flourish. It's not about one person's happiness being more important than the other's, but rather *both individuals contributing equally to the happiness of the partnership*. You can redefine success in your relationship and create a fulfilling, joyful partnership that allows both individuals to thrive.

When it comes to redefining relationship success, it's important to understand that success means different things for different types of relationships, and different things for different people. Whether it's a romantic, platonic, or familial relationship, success is all about setting the right expectations and goals. Here are some examples of what success might look like in each type of relationship:

Romantic Relationships

For romantic relationships, success is often measured by the level of connection and intimacy between partners. This includes emotional intimacy, physical intimacy, and communication. Some common goals for romantic relationships might include building a deep emotional bond, cultivating a strong physical connection, and creating a safe and supportive space for one another.

Platonic Relationships

In platonic relationships, success is often measured by the level of trust and support. Some common goals for platonic relationships might include building a strong foundation of trust and mutual support, fostering a sense of community and belonging, and creating meaningful memories together. This includes being a source of emotional support for one another during difficult times, celebrating each other's successes, and having fun together.

Familial Relationships

For familial relationships, success is often measured by the level of closeness and understanding between family members. This includes maintaining healthy communication, sharing values and traditions, and supporting one another through life's ups and downs. Some common goals for familial relationships might include building a strong sense of connection and belonging, fostering a culture of mutual respect and understanding, and creating a safe and nurturing environment for all family members.

It's important to acknowledge that not all relationships will fit neatly into these categories or meet these idealized definitions of success. Some of us may long for deeper connections or healthier dynamics than what we currently experience. If you find yourself in this position, remember that this too is part of your journey. Rather than viewing your current situation as a failure, you can choose to see it as an opportunity for growth and self-discovery.

The most powerful step you can take is to focus on your relationship with yourself first. By developing self-love, establishing healthy boundaries, and clarifying your values, you create the foundation for attracting and nurturing the meaningful relationships you desire. *Success isn't about having perfect relationships right now—it's about consistently moving toward more authentic and fulfilling connections, starting with yourself.*

Exercise for Self-Discovery: Redefining Relationship Success

1. Reflect on Your Definition of Success: Take a moment to write down what you *currently believe success looks like* in your relationships. This might include specific goals, feelings, or expectations. Be as detailed as possible.

2. Get Curious: Go through each item on your list and ask yourself the following questions:

- Is this truly my definition of success, or is it influenced by someone else (family, friends, society)?

- Does this expectation feel authentic to me, or does it feel imposed?

3. Rewrite Your Success: For any items that don't feel like they genuinely represent your version of success, rewrite them in a way that feels true to you. Use language that resonates with your values and desires. For example, if you originally wrote "always being happy together," you might revise it to "supporting each other through ups and downs while finding joy in everyday moments."

4. Set Intentions: Once you have your new definition of success, think about how you can begin to embody this in your relationships. What small actions or shifts can you implement to align your experience with this new definition?

5. Review and Reflect: Periodically revisit your list and adjust it as needed. Relationships evolve, and so will your understanding of what success means to you.

By taking the time to redefine what success looks like in your relationships, you create a clear roadmap for your journey. This empowers you to cultivate connections that truly fulfill you and reflect who you are at your core (love!).

No matter what type of relationship you're in, the key to redefining success is to focus on building strong, healthy connections with the people in your life. This means setting clear expectations, communicating openly and honestly, and being willing to grow and change together. Remember, relationships are not static—they are constantly evolving and changing—and success is about being flexible and adaptable as you navigate the ups and downs of life together.

CHAPTER TWENTY-EIGHT

Redefining Intimacy

INTIMACY IS A CRUCIAL aspect of any relationship, extending far beyond physical connection. True intimacy emerges when two whole, happy people come together, creating space for mutual growth and evolution. It's about embarking on a shared journey of discovery, both individually and as a team. **The real "chemistry" happens when two people who love themselves find one another** and create an environment of authenticity, connection, and mutual respect.

Reigniting Passion Within Your Relationship

So, what does it take to maintain connection and reignite the passion within your relationship? Here are a few key elements to consider:

Create Safety

A key aspect of safety in intimacy is the ability to say no without fear of repercussions. Consent isn't just about saying yes—it's about having the freedom to say no and having that boundary respected completely. Intimacy means honoring both your own boundaries and your partner's—it's never about pushing through discomfort or expecting others to do so. When both partners prioritize mutual comfort and respect, it creates a foundation for authentic expression and deeper connection.

Make Time for Play and Adventure

Intimacy thrives on novelty and excitement, so it's important to make time for play and adventure in your relationship. This could mean trying new things together, going on spontaneous trips, or simply setting aside dedicated time to have fun and connect with each other, both emotionally and physically. Need some fresh ideas? Check out the *10 Fun Ways to Connect with Intention* PDF guide on loveunstuck.com for inspiration—from cooking adventures to outdoor excursions, you'll find creative ways to spark joy and deepen your bond. As they say, "couples that play together, stay together!"

Make Space for Pleasure

Understanding Desire

Pleasure is a crucial component to creating healthy connected relationships, and not-so-coincidentally one of the biggest conflicts many couples face. A great deal of frustration and disappointment can arise through misunderstanding how pleasure (enjoying) and desire (wanting) works—it is different for everyone—and through expecting others to function in the same ways as we do. Spoiler alert: they don't.

Creating Safety and Consent

The foundation of pleasure in healthy relationships is that experiences must be enjoyable for all parties involved. Everyone needs to feel safe to say no at any time without repercussions—*consent isn't just sexy, it's essential.*

Exploring Different Forms of Pleasure

Remember that pleasure extends beyond sexual connection. It might include:

- Emotional intimacy through deep conversations

- Physical comfort through non-sexual touch

- Shared joy in activities and adventures

- Simple moments of connection and presence

Building Trust Through Boundaries

When we honor differing boundaries and preferences around pleasure, we create deeper trust and connection. This trust allows for more authentic expression of desires and needs over time, resulting in many more opportunities to enjoy pleasure.

Embrace Uncomfortable Conversations

Uncomfortable conversations are inevitable in any relationship, but it's how we handle them that matters. When it comes to physical intimacy, we want to avoid sweeping uncomfortable issues under the rug, instead making an effort to approach these challenging topics in a healthy, productive way. This means actively listening to each other, staying curious and open-minded, and working together to find a resolution that works for both of you, both in *and* out of the bedroom.

Take Responsibility for Yourself

In order to maintain a strong connection with your partner, it's essential to take complete responsibility for yourself and your contribution to the relationship. This means accepting *what is*, moving forward from an empowered position, and being willing to work on your own personal growth and evolution.

Stay Curious and Open

Relationships are constantly evolving, and it's important to stay curious and open to each other's growth and changes. Following our curiosity also keeps us from making assumptions and judgments along the way. If you want to create healthy, happy, and passionate relationships you must be willing to learn and grow together, ask vulnerable questions, and stay open to exploring new perspectives, beliefs, ideas and experiences.

Communicate Freely

One of the signposts of a healthy relationship is feeling safe to "get naked" emotionally: to speak up, ask for what you need, and express your feelings openly and honestly. This means avoiding assumptions, asking for clarity when needed, and ensuring that both partners feel heard and understood.

When sharing your needs, it can be immensely helpful to also share your intention or explain why you need something. This additional context can greatly improve understanding between partners. By providing the *why* behind our needs, we invite our partners into our inner world, fostering deeper connection and empathy.

When it comes to your partner's needs, seeking clarity rather than making assumptions (about what they mean) or judgments (about what they are thinking or why they acted) may feel as vulnerable as being physically naked, but it will significantly reduce conflict and increase both empathy and intimacy. We have the opportunity to both *see our partner* and to *be seen*—if we are brave enough to risk the vulnerability. This mutual understanding, built on clear communication of needs and intentions, creates a foundation for a relationship where both partners feel truly heard, valued, and supported.

Bringing it All Together

Incorporating these elements into your relationship routine will help you to cultivate a deeper intimacy that will keep your relationship strong and thriving, even during challenging times. Remember, intimacy is not just about sex! It's about creating a space where both partners can feel supported in their personal growth and evolution. It's about connection and communication. It's about co-regulation of our nervous systems—working as a team to navigate challenges from a calm and conscious state of being. It's about an energetic exchange. Intimacy is about so many amazing things—physical intimacy is just the cherry on the cake (all the puns intended)!

I remember more than one time when I simply couldn't bring myself to be affectionate with a partner. The emotional distance between us made being more affectionate feel impossible. Through this experience, I learned that rebuilding connection requires patience, and that it starts with creating emotional safety first. Small steps like having honest conversations about feelings, practicing non-sexual touch, and rebuilding trust through consistent respect of boundaries can help bridge that gap. This journey taught me that reconnecting isn't about forcing intimacy—it's about creating the conditions where intimacy can naturally flourish.

Just as deepening intimacy requires openness to exploration, cultivating curiosity can transform how we approach our relationships. Let's explore how this powerful mindset can enhance every aspect of our connections.

Go Deeper

For a deeper understanding of sexuality and connection, check out these illuminating reads: *Come as You Are: The Surprising New Science That Will Transform Your Sex Life* and *Come Together: The Science (and Art!) of Creating Lasting Sexual Connections* both by Emily Nagoski, Ph.D.

Whether you are currently in a relationship or not, these books offer valuable insights into understanding desire, pleasure, and creating lasting sexual connections.

CHAPTER TWENTY-NINE

Curiosity is Key

As you navigate the ups and downs of your relationship, curiosity can be a key tool in your toolkit. By approaching your thoughts and emotions with a curious and non-judgmental mindset, you can gain a greater awareness of what's really going on inside of you and between you and your partner.

When we're in survival mode, our thoughts and emotions can easily spiral out of control, leading us to react in ways that aren't always helpful or productive. *By approaching situations with curiosity rather than judgment, we can better understand the root of these reactions and respond more intentionally.* For example, let's consider Mia, who often found herself feeling frustrated and misunderstood in her relationship with her partner, Alex. When conflicts arose, Mia would typically respond defensively, leading to heated arguments that left both partners feeling hurt and disconnected. It wasn't until Mia opened herself to curiosity that everything began to change.

Initially skeptical, Mia decided to give it a shot. During a particularly tense moment, instead of reacting immediately, she paused and asked herself, "What am I really feeling right now? What is Alex experiencing?" This simple shift in mindset allowed her to step back from the emotional chaos and approach the situation with a sense of curiosity rather than judgment.

To deepen her understanding, Mia started journaling daily, reflecting on her thoughts and emotions related to her relationship. One day, she noticed a recurring theme: she often felt insecure when Alex would express their opinions strongly. Rather than assuming Alex was being dismissive, Mia began to explore how her own insecurities were shaping her reactions. This insight prompted Mia to ask Alex more open-ended questions during their conversations, inviting deeper discussions about their feelings and perspectives.

Mia's journey into curiosity not only transformed her internal landscape but also fostered a more empathetic dialogue with Alex. By approaching their relationship with a willingness to explore rather than react, Mia created a safe space for both of them to share their thoughts and emotions without fear of judgment. This newfound openness led to increased intimacy and understanding, allowing Mia and Alex to grow together rather than apart.

Journaling is a particularly powerful tool for cultivating curiosity. By setting aside time each day to reflect on your thoughts and emotions, you can gain greater clarity and insight into what's really going on beneath the surface. You may find it helpful to focus on one area at a time, deeply exploring your thoughts and feelings about it before moving on to the next.

Through her commitment to curiosity, Mia learned that by observing her feelings without rushing to conclusions, she could defuse tension and cultivate a stronger connection with her partner. This experience exemplifies how **curiosity can unlock deeper understanding and compassion, paving the way for a healthier, more fulfilling relationship.**

By becoming actively curious, you can release judgment, ask questions rather than make assumptions, and listen rather than jumping to fix-it mode. This can help you remove the defensive and disproportionate reactions that can often lead to conflict and hurt in relationships. With a more objective and curious mindset, you can approach your relationship with greater understanding, compassion, and openness, creating space for growth and connection.

Go Deeper

Ready to explore your relationship with curiosity? I've created a set of thought-provoking journaling prompts designed to deepen your self-discovery journey. Download these printable prompts at loveunstuck.com and begin uncovering new insights about your relationships.

Want to take your journaling practice further? Check out my *Unstuck for Women Daily Self Discovery Journal* to start your 90 day guided daily reflection and transformation!

CHAPTER THIRTY

Reframing Limiting Beliefs and Mindsets

OUR BELIEFS AND MINDSETS are running in the background, influencing our relationships *every single fucking day*—often without our awareness. Many of these beliefs were ingrained during our early childhood and continue to affect our perception of the world, defining what's "right or wrong," "good or bad," and how we view ourselves and others. To create lasting change, we must first become aware of these beliefs and mindsets to determine if they genuinely serve us and our relationships.

You have the power to change your life. You don't need to wait for the perfect moment, and you certainly don't need to wait for anyone else to change before you embark on your journey of transforming your life. It all starts with one small step—a single decision to *take charge of your life*. Every small step forward, no matter how seemingly insignificant, sets you on the path of growth and transformation.

It is your thoughts, beliefs, and mindsets that shape your reality. They influence your body's stress responses and color your lived experiences. Your beliefs about your own identity, even if they aren't objectively true, significantly impact how you interact with yourself and the world.

Understanding how change happens is crucial. I call my transformational system the CREATE Method, and it starts with Calibrating Your Consciousness. Through this method, we examine how our thoughts, beliefs, and mindsets shape our reality, influencing our body's stress responses and coloring our lived experiences.

Here's where it gets tricky: your brain, with its remarkable efficiency, prefers to keep you on autopilot, embracing the familiar and resisting change. It's a natural defense mechanism to keep you safe and comfortable, but it can also hinder your progress when it comes to breaking free from self-limiting beliefs.

Remember, the Reticular Activating System (RAS) does not look at what is good or best for us, *it acts only to keep us safe*. It does its job by keeping our experience in line with those already-held beliefs and mindsets, because to our RAS: **what is familiar is safe, and what is uncertain is unsafe**. And as you know, when you desire to grow, you must be willing to step outside of the familiar and face uncertainty. This requires intentional work to look at the actual results and function of our beliefs and mindsets, both conscious and unconscious.

Most often, when you are unable to create lasting change in your life, it's because on some level you are benefiting from the status quo. Sometimes these "benefits" can be pretty sneaky, and often are no longer actually benefits at all.

Let's explore this concept with some examples:

- If you don't believe you're worthy of love, you may unconsciously self-sabotage relationships, pushing away affection because deep down, you don't feel deserving of it. To your brain, you are doing this to protect yourself from the potential pain of love lost. As if!

- Or maybe you believe the myth that you will feel good once you have someone to "complete" you—you approach love with the belief that you're missing something and that you are separate from what you "need"—and, as a result, you are always waiting for someone else to make you feel good.

In both scenarios, despite your best intentions, you end up preserving the current identity you have created for yourself (that you're unworthy and incomplete).

The key thing to recognize here is that this problem is not about some objective truth—it's actually about what *you believe to be true*. When your actions align with the identity you hold, it becomes much easier to change habits for the long haul. While it might feel safer to guard your heart, it's definitely not going to lead to the outcomes that you want the most.

So, how can you create lasting change from the inside out? **It's time to shift your identity.** Start by examining your mindsets, beliefs, stories, and excuses. Are they supporting the person you want to be? If not, challenge them. Shake off the beliefs that are keeping you stuck—literally shake them loose from your body to create space for new beliefs! It's time to replace self-doubt with self-empowerment, fear with courage, and limitations with possibilities.

As you embrace your new identity, aligning your thoughts and beliefs with your desired Self, you'll witness the magic of transformation unfold. Habits that once seemed elusive will now find their place in your life, finally sticking around for the long term.

Additionally, we must remember that our perspective will never be exactly the same as anyone else's. No one—not even *one* of the almost 8.2 billion humans currently inhabiting the planet—has had the same experiences you have had. **This always leaves room for possibility and for different interpretations of the same situation.**

Perhaps you, like my client whom I'll call "Jenn," have some insecurities that are significantly impacting your relationship. And perhaps you, dear reader, have also felt unattractive and undesirable, just like Jenn did. I trust that you will find the hope you long for in her story.

Now let me start this by saying that Jenn is the kind of woman who radiates warmth and kindness to everyone she meets. When we first met, she spoke confidently and she had a pretty clear idea of what she wanted out of life, yet something was missing, and she was on a mission to find "it."

To the outside world, Jenn appeared confident and composed, but deep inside, she was wrestling with a shadow of self-doubt, poor body image and low self-esteem. She told me that her loving husband would often shower her with compliments, praising her beauty, intelligence, and unique charm. She was, according to him, "irresistible, hot and sexy;" he regularly told her so. But Jenn was perplexed.

The truth was, her husband's words were everything she thought that she wanted to hear, yet instead of basking in his loving and affectionate attention, she struggled to accept his words. Doubtful thoughts danced in her mind, whispering, "Why would he see anything special in me?" and "I don't feel sexy, he probably just wants sex." She couldn't help but wonder if he was just saying what he thought she wanted to hear, and she told him as much.

Jenn's insecurities had really cast a gloomy cloud over her relationship, not to mention her overall mood. In intimate moments, she couldn't let go and truly connect with her husband because her mind was constantly preoccupied with negative thoughts about her physical appearance. She found it nearly impossible to believe that he genuinely found her attractive and desirable and yet he was still there, consistently showing her how much he loved and appreciated her.

After years of feeling trapped in this cycle, Jenn knew something had to change. She had finally come to the conclusion that if she was going to find whatever was "missing" in her life, it was going to be up to her to find it. Thus began her journey of self-discovery and transformation.

For her entire adult life, Jenn had been wearing masks to hide her vulnerabilities, struggling to fit into a mold of perceived perfection. It clearly hadn't been working so she pulled up her "big girl panties" and finally mustered up the courage required to do things differently. It was time for Jenn to shed those masks and embrace her authentic self once and for all.

Through self-reflection and guided support, Jenn began to challenge her negative beliefs rather than simply accept them. With a bit of practice, she even learned to receive and accept compliments with gratitude and grace! With time and patience, she slowly peeled off the masks she had been hiding behind, revealing the real, vulnerable, and beautiful woman beneath. Things really started to click for her when she started to recognize that her husband's view of her might indeed be very different from her own distorted self-perception.

Together, we customized a set of strategies based on the CREATE Method that Jenn incorporated into her daily routine. Every time negative thoughts arose, she challenged them using The Spiral Stopper Method detailed in *Unstuck for Women*. She built a toolbox full of the strategies, finding that conscious breath, affirmations and mental rehearsal worked best for stopping her spirals.

Her transformation deepened when she finally confided in her husband about her internal struggles. To her complete surprise, his response was pure love and support. He shared how she was a real gift in his life, filling his days with love and joy, and his unwavering support became a guiding light on her journey of self-discovery. In time, her husband even began to share more of *his* more vulnerable side with her and as a result, the spark in their relationship reignited. Over time, they grew even closer, connecting on a deeper, more meaningful level.

But Jenn's transformation didn't stop there. With each step forward, her confidence blossomed like a flower in full bloom. She radiated a newfound sense of self-assurance that caught the attention of everyone around her—her friends all wanted to know where her bold new confidence came from. And the magic of Jenn's transformation extended well beyond her romantic relationship. Her self-confidence positively influenced her relationships with her children, family, friends, and coworkers. Her transformation became most apparent one sunny afternoon at the beach with her family. As they built sandcastles and splashed in the waves, Jenn couldn't help but notice that for the first time, she had been truly present, and that her beach experience had been free of her usual self-judgment. It was in those precious moments with her family when Jenn realized that by being her true self, she had unlocked the key to authentic happiness.

Through her dedication to re-patterning her beliefs and mindsets, Jenn discovered a newfound sense of liberation and joy. She learned to embrace her body, not as society's definition of perfection, but as a vessel of love having human experiences. It is safe to say that Jenn's entire life changed when she truly understood the true power of self-compassion and self-acceptance. She learned to celebrate her strengths and accept her "imperfections," realizing that they were actually part of what made her beautifully unique. She realized that true confidence didn't come from seeking approval from others but rather from accepting and loving herself unconditionally.

Jenn's journey shows us that the most profound transformations start from within. By challenging our limiting beliefs and embracing our authentic selves, we unlock a world of possibilities and create space for more meaningful connections. When we step into unconditional self-love and acceptance, we discover that we are capable of creating the relationships we truly desire.

CHAPTER THIRTY-ONE

What you Resist Persists

HAVE YOU EVER TRIED to resist feeling a certain way, only to find that the more you try to avoid it, the more it persists? This is because where our attention goes, our energy flows. The more we focus on avoiding uncomfortable emotions, the more power we actually give them to remain in our lives. In doing so, we in fact *hold onto those emotions and experiences that we do not want*, rather than moving through them. **Although it may seem counterintuitive, to truly let go and move forward, we need to stop resisting and start exploring.**

In a relationship, it is not uncommon to find yourself resisting uncomfortable emotions that arise from your interactions with your partner. Perhaps you try to avoid conflict or suppress your feelings in an effort to keep the peace. Unfortunately, these emotions will persist—growing stronger the more you resist them.

Instead, try getting curious about your emotions, thoughts, and patterns. Take a step back and observe them with a non-judgmental attitude. Once you understand them better, you can choose how to respond. When faced with uncomfortable emotions or situations in your relationship, remember that you have four choices:

- **Avoid it**: This is a tempting option, but it will only lead to more discomfort in the long run.

- **Accept it as is**: This may mean acknowledging that the situation is uncomfortable but choosing to remain present and engaged with it.

- **Release it:** Let go of the uncomfortable emotion or reframe it in a more positive light.

- **Take action to change it:** If the uncomfortable emotion is pointing to an issue that needs to be addressed, take appropriate action to resolve it.

Similar to shifting out of problem-seeking mode and into solution-seeking mode (which we will discuss further in Chapter 36), **setting your energy and focus on *what you do want* is in fact the fastest way to attain it**. By accepting and releasing uncomfortable emotions, you can create more space for positive experiences and deeper connection in your relationship.

Exercise to Release Resistance: The Work—Reframing Your Beliefs

This exercise is inspired by Byron Katie's work, which emphasizes the power of questioning our beliefs and thoughts. I invite you to explore how you might be arguing with reality (*what is*) and use the process below to shift your perspective.

1. Identify the Thought: Write down a specific thought or belief related to an uncomfortable emotion or situation in your relationship. For example, "My partner never listens to me," or "I'm always the one who compromises."

2. Ask the Four Questions: Reflect on the thought using the following four questions:

- **Is it true?** Take a moment to consider whether this belief is an absolute truth. Is it always the case?

- **Can you absolutely know that it's true?** Dig deeper. Can you find *any evidence* that contradicts this belief?

- **How do you react, and what happens, when you believe that thought?** Observe how this belief affects your feelings and actions. What emotions arise? How do you behave towards your partner or yourself?

- **Who would you be without that thought?** Imagine your life and relationship without this belief. How would you feel? How would you act?

3. Turn It Around: After reflecting on the four questions, turn the original thought around to create a new perspective. For example, if your original thought was, "My partner never listens to me," you could turn it around to:

- "I am not listening to my partner."

- "I sometimes don't express my needs clearly."

- "My partner does listen to me in other ways."

4. Find Specific Examples: For each turnaround, write down specific examples of how this new perspective is true in your life. This can help reinforce the shift in thinking. For instance:

- "I am not listening to my partner when I'm busy with my phone."

- "When I express my needs clearly, I feel more heard."

5. Practice and Reflect: Over the next week, keep your original thought and its turnarounds in mind. Notice how they affect your feelings and interactions with your partner. Reflect on any changes you observe in your relationship dynamics.

6. Journal Your Insights: Write about your experiences and insights during this process. What did you learn about yourself and your relationship? How can you continue to apply this practice moving forward?

By using this exercise, you'll cultivate greater awareness of your beliefs and how they influence your emotions and actions. Reframing your thoughts can help you create a more compassionate understanding of yourself and your partner, paving the way for deeper connection and growth.

When we stop resisting *what is* and start exploring our thoughts and emotions with curiosity, we create space for real transformation. Remember, what you resist truly does persist—but **what you embrace and accept, you can transform**. By questioning our beliefs and remaining open to new perspectives, we free ourselves from the grip of limiting thoughts and emotions. This freedom allows us to show up more authentically in our relationships, creating deeper connections based on true understanding rather than resistance. The next time you find yourself pushing against uncomfortable emotions or situations, pause and ask yourself: *What might change if I stopped resisting and got curious instead?*

While learning to stop resisting and start exploring is crucial, we need effective tools to express these discoveries. This is where conscious communication becomes essential.

CHAPTER THIRTY-TWO

Improving Communication

EFFECTIVE COMMUNICATION IS THE foundation of any healthy and successful relationship; without it you're in trouble. Good communication is about being honest, open, and vulnerable with your partner while also staying curious and non-judgmental.

When conflicts arise, it's important to work together as a team to find a solution that works for both parties.

Before engaging in any important conversation, it's crucial to create a safe space by regulating your nervous system. Think of your nervous system as the conductor of an orchestra, setting the tempo and tuning all the instruments together. When your nervous system is out of balance, your communications can easily become off key.

Let's explore some simple exercises designed to help you regulate your nervous system, which will be instrumental (pun intended) in preparing for healthy communication and interaction.

Exercises for Self-Regulation: Communication Harmony

Here are some self-regulation tools to help you maintain harmony:

1. Deep breathing: This is an incredible tool because you can use it anywhere, anytime. Before an important conversation, pause to take three deep breaths, focusing solely on the air coming into your body and leaving your body.

2. Box breathing: Inhale for four counts, hold for four counts, exhale for four counts, and hold for four counts. Repeat this cycle three times to ground yourself.

3. Meditation or mindfulness practices: These can help keep you calm and move through survival mode, allowing you to respond consciously rather than react emotionally. You might enjoy using the *Creating Love Sweary AF Meditation* on my website (loveunstuck.com), to cultivate a loving mental state perfect for productive communication.

By regulating your nervous system, you create space for conscious creation—choosing with intention how you want to respond.

Effective communication is much like a dance, where both partners need to feel and flow with the music, moving together fluidly. Otherwise, someone's basically just stepping on the other's toes.

Preparing for Conversation

Now that you have tools to regulate your nervous system and create that essential foundation of calm, let's look at how to prepare for important conversations. Just like an athlete wouldn't jump into a competition without warming up, we shouldn't dive into significant discussions without proper preparation.

1. Choose the right timing: Ensure you're not hungry, angry, tired, stressed out, worried, or distracted.

2. Mentally rehearse the conversation: Visualize a calm setting where you're both open to hearing and seeing one another.

3. Set clear intentions: Reflect on what you hope to achieve from this conversation. Is it a deeper understanding? Are you seeking to apologize? Are you trying to have a deeper connection?

4. Practice articulating your thoughts: You can do this out loud, with a friend, or even record yourself—and adjust your tone, pace, and body language as needed.

Approaching conversations with a lens of love rather than fear can transform interactions from a defensive battle into an opportunity for deeper connection. **Before you speak, remind yourself that**

you wish to see your partner with compassion and curiosity, with an open and accepting perspective.

Common Communication Challenges

Now that we know how to best prepare for effective communication, let's look at some common communication challenges faced in relationships. In the table below are seven examples of communication pitfalls and how you can avoid them to improve the way you communicate within all your relationships.

Table 32-1: Communication Pitfalls and How to Avoid Them

Communication Pitfall	Why This is a Pitfall	How to Improve Communication
Making Assumptions	Deciding you know what your partner is thinking or feeling can lead to miscommunication and hurt feelings.	Ask clarifying questions* to get the information you are unsure about, and practice active listening** to gain a better understanding of another's perspectives.
Defensiveness	Rushing in to defend yourself when your partner expresses their feelings or opinions can shut down communication and escalate conflict.	This is another opportunity for active listening. Try to approach the conversation with a gentle curiosity and a willingness to hear their point of view. Ask clarifying questions to understand their perspective. We will address triggers in more depth in the next chapter.
Stonewalling	Withdrawing, refusing to respond, or shutting down during a conversation can make your partner feel unheard and dismissed.	Take a break during difficult conversations if you need to but commit to returning to the conversation when you are ready to engage in a productive way.

Criticism	Describing your partner's behavior or character in a disapproving way can be hurtful and damage their self-esteem (and with it, your connection).	Instead, focus on specific behaviors that are causing problems and communicate your feelings and needs in a non-judgmental way, without making it about their character.
Invalidating feelings	Dismissing or minimizing your partner's feelings can make them feel unheard and unsupported.	Validate their feelings and express empathy, even if you don't necessarily agree with their perspective.
Interrupting	Interrupting your partner while they are speaking can make them feel disrespected and unheard.	Practice active listening and wait for them to finish before responding.
Gaslighting	This form of emotional abuse involves denying or twisting events, experiences or conversations to make the victim question their memory, perception of reality and, as a result, even their sanity.	When gaslighting is present, communication can become rather tricky. To improve communication when gaslighting is present, focus first on maintaining your sense of reality by documenting events and trusting your own perceptions of them. Set clear boundaries, use "I" statements to express your feelings, and be willing to disengage from unproductive conversations. Seek support from a trusted professional when needed.

Definitions:

***CLARIFYING QUESTIONS**

Clarifying questions are essential for eliminating judgment and assumptions in communication, opening conversations to gain deeper insights into others' perspectives and experiences. They help us suspend our own limiting viewpoints that might create inaccurate narratives, instead encouraging a more open and understanding dialogue.

By asking questions like "What did you mean by...?" or "Can you please tell me more about...?", we create space for others to elaborate on their thoughts and feelings, promoting active listening and challenging our own assumptions. This approach allows us to step outside our limited perspective, avoid misunderstandings, and learn from the diverse experiences of those around us.

****ACTIVE LISTENING**

Active listening is a crucial communication skill that involves being fully present and attentive to another person's message, with the intention of increasing understanding, gaining clarity, and deepening connection. It requires an openness to hear others without judgment, setting aside our own preconceptions.

A key component of active listening is paraphrasing, repeating back our understanding of what was said in our own words to check for accuracy. This practice might involve saying, "So what I'm hearing is..." or "Let me see if I've understood correctly..." By doing this, we not only confirm our comprehension but also demonstrate our engagement and give the speaker an opportunity to clarify any misunderstandings, ultimately fostering a more meaningful and empathetic exchange.

Let's see how these pitfalls might play out in a real situation. Leah and Mike's story illustrates how quickly communication can break down—and how it can be rebuilt. When Leah came home tired from work and saw dishes in the sink, she immediately snapped, "You never help around here!" (criticism). Mike, feeling attacked, responded, "I do plenty around here, you just never notice!" (defensiveness). Leah rolled her eyes and walked away (stonewalling), while Mike assumed she was being unreasonable because she was stressed about work (making assumptions).

Later, after both had regulated their nervous systems, they tried again. This time, Leah expressed, "I'm feeling overwhelmed with housework. When I see dishes in the sink after a long day, I feel unsupported" (replacing criticism with feelings). Mike practiced active listening and asked clarifying questions: "I hear you feeling overwhelmed. Can you help me understand what would make you feel more supported?" This opened up a productive dialogue about sharing household responsibilities, demonstrating how shifting away from communication pitfalls can transform conflict into connection.

By identifying those pesky communication pitfalls, we can consider both where we have fallen into the trap of using them, as well as see what aspects of communication with others we find the most challenging. This allows us to step into more authentic communication styles. Below are some key tips for improving authentic communication in your relationships.

Stay Curious and Release Judgement

One of the biggest roadblocks to effective communication is judgment. When we judge our partners, we are less likely to truly listen to what they are saying and more likely to jump to conclusions or make assumptions. By staying curious and asking questions instead of assuming, we can better understand our partner's perspective and needs.

Listen, Don't Fix

Often, when our partner comes to us with a problem or concern, our first instinct is to try to fix it. However, sometimes our partner just needs to be heard and validated. *A good communicator listens more than they speak and will seek to understand before interjecting with their own opinions or solutions.*

When we constantly try to fix our partner's problems, the underlying message we are sending is that we see them as incapable of fixing their own problems. To avoid this pitfall, you may consider asking your partner what it is that they require from you: Do they want you to help them to problem-solve? Or do they just want to be heard? Then, respond from the desired perspective. By simply listening first, we can strengthen our emotional connection and build trust.

Communicate Honestly and Openly

Honesty is the backbone of any healthy relationship. It can be difficult to be vulnerable and share your innermost thoughts and feelings, but it is important to do so in order to build a strong foundation of trust. Be open and honest with your partner about your thoughts, feelings, and needs.

Finding Your Voice and Asking for What You Want

Finding your voice and asking for what you want can be challenging, especially if you are used to putting others' needs before your own. But it's important to remember that your needs are just as important as your partner's. *By clearly communicating your needs and desires, you give your partner the opportunity to support you and help you meet those needs.*

Dealing with Conflict

Conflict is inevitable in any relationship. However, *it's how we deal with conflict that determines the outcome.* When conflicts arise, try to approach the situation as a team. Focus on finding a solution that works for both of you, rather than trying to "win" the argument. Remember to stay calm, listen to your partner's perspective, and express your own needs in a respectful way. We will explore dealing with conflict in more depth in Chapter 34.

Learn How to Receive

Learning how to receive is just as important as learning how to give. Sometimes, we can be so focused on giving to others that we forget to allow ourselves to receive. Be open to receiving help, love, and support from your partner. *It's not a sign of weakness to ask for help or to receive it—it's a sign of strength.* Practice being open and vulnerable with your partner and allow yourself to receive the love and support they offer.

Here's the real deal on communication: Active listening, empathy, and open-mindedness are your trusty sidekicks on this adventure. Embrace them as the true superheroes that they are and watch how they transform the understanding between you and your partner.

By incorporating the tips in this chapter into your communication style, you can improve your emotional intelligence and build stronger, more fulfilling relationships. Remember, communication takes practice and patience, but the benefits are well worth the effort.

So, grab your communication toolkit, filled with compassion, curiosity, and a sprinkle of humor—we all need a good laugh sometimes!—because from now on, creating deep and meaningful connections is your new superpower!

CHAPTER THIRTY-THREE

Triggers as Teachers

FROM TIME TO TIME, you are likely to experience autonomic nervous system responses to something or someone else. The word "trigger" is so common that it seems divorced from what it is. **I would define a trigger as an intense emotional and/or physical reaction, to a word, sound, scent, image, or situation that instantly takes us back to a past trauma—triggers are an activation.** I prefer the term "activation" over "trigger" because it better describes what's actually happening—our nervous system is being activated, and this activation provides us with valuable information.

When you are "triggered" (activated), your response may catch you off guard or induce a spiral. I want you to know that *this is completely normal!* As conscious creators, we can choose to flip the script on being triggered to being activated when we put on our observer hats. **Triggers are information that is being brought to your attention to teach you something about yourself.**

When we experience an activation of this kind, it's important to remember that these experiences are simply bringing things to our awareness so that we can take a closer look at them. *Until we attach meaning, stories, beliefs, and emotion to them, these "triggers" are just neutral pieces of information.* This is a powerful realization because it means that we have the power to shape our responses and interpretations.

To deal with these activations effectively, it's crucial to interrupt the spiral of negative thoughts and emotions. I've developed a technique called The Spiral Stopper Method, which I detail in my book *Unstuck for Women*. This method allows us to step back and observe our responses with childlike curiosity, free from judgment. By simply noticing what's happening within us, we can gain valuable insights from these self-reflective teachers we have come to call "triggers." While this process may feel challenging at first, with consistent practice it will become second nature, empowering you to respond to these activations more consciously and constructively.

Triggers in relationships can be valuable sources of information that provide opportunities for personal growth and deeper understanding. (Yes, *personal* growth, those triggers are all about YOU, not about anyone or anything else!)

Common Triggers as Opportunities for Growth

Below are some examples of common triggers that people experience in relationships and some suggestions for how you can turn these "challenges" into opportunities for growth.

Jealousy and Insecurity

Feeling jealous or insecure when your partner interacts with others, especially someone you perceive as a threat, can be emotionally activating. Instead of suppressing these feelings, use them as a signal to explore your own insecurities and fears.

- Ask yourself why you feel this way and what underlying beliefs or past experiences might be influencing your reaction.

- By exploring the root of your jealousy, you can address any unresolved issues and build greater trust and confidence in both you and your relationship. Talk about a win-win!

Feeling Ignored or Undervalued

When you feel ignored or undervalued by your partner, it can stir up emotions of disappointment and resentment. Instead of letting these feelings fester and grow, use them as an opportunity to practice honest, assertive communication.

- Express your feelings and needs to your partner (in a non-accusatory manner), providing them with an opportunity to understand your perspective.

- This hot button of unmet needs can lead to deeper emotional connection and empathy, strengthening your bond as you learn to validate each other's feelings.

Disagreements

When you and your partner have different opinions or priorities, it can be easy to get stuck in an argument. But if you can shift your perspective and see the disagreement as an opportunity to learn from each other, you can deepen your understanding and respect for one another.

- Remember, you're on the same team and when one of you loses a fight, you both lose.

- When you take the time to truly listen and understand, you'll often discover a new perspective or find a compromise that works for both of you.

Triggers from Past Relationships

Sometimes, something your partner says or does can re-activate a painful memory or feeling from a past relationship.

- Rather than reacting based on that past experience, try to communicate honestly with your partner about what's really going on for you.

- You never know, they might even be able to offer the support and understanding needed as you heal from those past wounds.

Lack of Quality Time

Feeling disconnected due to a lack of quality time with your partner can cause a powerful emotional reaction. This emotional activation may cause you to get upset and withdraw, further reinforcing the feeling of disconnection.

- Use this emotional reaction as a chance to prioritize your relationship and explore meaningful ways to spend time together.

- Plan date nights or activities that nurture your emotional connection and allow for open communication, reinforcing the importance of your bond. Need some inspiration? Visit loveunstuck.com and grab the *10 Fun Ways to Connect with Intention* PDF guide.

Fear of Abandonment

If you have a deep-seated fear of being abandoned or rejected, it can be difficult to fully trust your partner. However, if you can recognize that fear and communicate about it with your partner, you just might be able to work together to build even greater security and trust in your relationship.

- Let this information support you to create routines or rituals that help you feel more connected and supported.

- Continue the work of building your own sense of self-worth and resilience.

In each of these examples, you can see that triggers are the teachers that provide necessary information to facilitate personal growth. By approaching these activations with curiosity, empathy, and a willingness to address underlying issues, you can use them as stepping-stones towards deeper intimacy, understanding, and personal development, all while saving yourself from a great deal of unnecessary pain and suffering.

Triggers in Non-Romantic Relationships

Of course, these emotional activations are not exclusive to our romantic relationships. Whether we're interacting with our children, colleagues, friends, or family members, our emotional responses provide valuable insights into our own needs, boundaries, and areas for growth. Just as in romantic relationships, these activations in other relationships serve as signposts, pointing us toward opportunities for deeper understanding and personal development. Let's explore some common examples.

Parent-Child Power Struggles

Parenting can be filled with triggers, especially when facing a battle of wills with your child. Instead of getting frustrated and resorting to attempts to control your child, aim to view these activations as invitations to practice patience and understanding. Reflect on your parenting style and consider whether there are more effective ways to communicate and set boundaries with your child, while maintaining connection as your key goal. Using the trigger as a chance for self-reflection can lead to a healthier parent-child dynamic.

Conflict with a Coworker

Conflicts with coworkers can be common in the workplace. Instead of avoiding or escalating a conflict situation, use it as an opportunity to practice your conflict resolution skills (we will explore these in greater depth in Chapter 34). Seek to understand the other person's perspective and be open to finding common ground. This activation can lead to improved communication and collaboration, fostering a more positive and productive work environment.

Arguments about Household Chores

Frequent arguments about household chores can be a common trigger for many couples and housemates alike. Instead of getting caught in a cycle of blame and frustration, view this activation as an opportunity to discuss deeper issues related to communication, expectations, and division of responsibilities. Use your emotional reaction as a starting point for open and honest conversations about one another's needs and preferences, finding compromises, and creating a more harmonious living environment.

Feeling Left Out by Friends

Feeling left out or excluded by friends can trigger emotional pain. Instead of withdrawing or harboring resentment, use this activation as an opportunity to explore your own feelings of self-worth and belonging. Engaging in open and honest conversations with your friends about your feelings can lead to deeper understanding and a stronger bond.

Boundary Setting with Friends

Sometimes, friends or acquaintances may infringe on our personal boundaries or make demands that create discomfort. Rather than avoiding confrontation, view this as a chance to practice assertiveness and boundary setting. Having open and honest conversations about our boundaries can feel scary, but these incredible activations contain within them the opportunity for an even deeper and more meaningful connection.

Comparison and Envy Amongst Peers

In competitive environments, comparison and envy may arise. Instead of allowing these triggers to breed negativity, use them as opportunities for self-reflection and growth. Identify your strengths and accomplishments, focusing on your personal progress rather than comparing yourself to others. Besides, you can only be jealous of someone else when *you don't believe you too can have it*—when you believe you can also have it, the very same activation becomes *inspiring*. This activation can lead to increased self-awareness and a healthier perspective on success and collaboration.

Remember, triggers are not inherently negative: they are valuable signals that can guide you toward areas of personal growth and self-awareness. **By embracing these activations with curiosity and a willingness to explore their underlying causes, we em-**

power ourselves to take control of our interpretation—and our responses. With practice, you too can transform these challenging moments into opportunities for positive change and deeper connection. The next time you find yourself activated, remember that triggers are merely teachers, and *you* have the power to choose how you respond.

CHAPTER THIRTY-FOUR

Navigating Conflict

CONFLICT IS A NATURAL part of any relationship—no matter how compatible you are, disagreements are bound to happen. However, the way you handle conflict can either bring you closer together or it can push you further apart.

Effective conflict resolution isn't just about managing our reactions, but also about expressing ourselves in ways that foster understanding and create respect. Here's how you can practice this:

1. Use compassionate communication: Start with affirmations or recognition of the other person's experiences and efforts. This helps to create a positive foundation for the conversation and shows that you acknowledge their challenges and perspectives.

2. Set boundaries: Define what respectful communication looks like for you. As you already know, healthy boundaries are an invitation into deeper connection with you. Clearly express your boundaries to your partner and kindly enforce them if they are crossed. We will talk further about how to create healthy boundaries in the following chapter.

3. Focus on the issue, not the person: Address the behavior or situation, not the character of your partner. Avoid "always" or "never" accusations and other forms of exaggeration, as these create defensive reactions.

4. Seek to understand: Ask clarifying questions to really understand where your partner is coming from. Assume the best intentions from your partner, even if something is being activated in you.

5. Validate feelings: Communicate in a way that validates your partner's feelings. Show compassion and share your perspective without overshadowing theirs. When people feel heard, they are much more inclined to work together as a team.

6. Create win-win solutions: Look for solutions that satisfy both parties. This might involve compromise, but seeking new outcomes often results in finding a completely new third path that works even better than either person's original idea.

As we explored in Chapter 16, your attachment style (anxious, avoidant, or secure) significantly impacts how you approach conflict. Let's look at how these patterns specifically show up during disagreements.

When securely attached partners face conflict, they tend to:

- Stay present and regulated during difficult conversations

- Express needs clearly while remaining open to their partner's perspective

- Trust in the strength of their connection even during disagreements

- Work together as a team to find solutions that work for both partners

This is the model we're aiming for, regardless of our current attachment style.

If you have an **anxious attachment style**, you may be more sensitive to potential relationship threats, struggle with emotional regulation, and need extra reassurance. Your fear of abandonment and rejection can make even minor disagreements feel threatening.

If you have an **avoidant attachment style**, you may tend to withdraw or shut down in response to conflict, prioritizing independence and emotional distance as protection. This can make it challenging to stay present and work through issues together, and you may need more space and time to process your emotions.

Understanding these conflict resolution strategies through the lens of attachment styles helps us apply them more effectively. For example, an anxiously attached person might need extra reassurance during the repair process, while an avoidant partner might need more space to process before engaging in repair. By recognizing these patterns, we can adapt our approach accordingly:

- If you or your partner has an anxious attachment style, build in extra reassurance and validation during conflict resolution

- If you or your partner has an avoidant attachment style, allow for processing time while maintaining connection

- If you're both securely attached, use your natural teamwork orientation to find solutions together

- If you have different styles, acknowledge and respect these differences while working toward secure functioning

The dance between different attachment styles can often play out as conflicts within a relationship. For example, if one partner has an anxious attachment style and the other has an avoidant attachment style, conflict may arise when the anxious partner seeks more reassurance and intimacy, while the avoidant partner may withdraw or feel overwhelmed.

It's important to understand that noting any differences in attachment style is not a personal attack—this is simply the sum of your unique life experiences and conditioning. By recognizing and accepting these differences, we can begin to navigate conflicts with compassion and understanding for ourselves and our partners.

For those with anxious attachment styles, it can be helpful to practice self-soothing techniques and communicate openly about your needs in a non-accusatory way. Those with avoidant attachment styles may benefit from setting boundaries and taking space when feeling overwhelmed, while also acknowledging your partner's need for intimacy.

Remember, it takes two to tango, and **navigating conflicts in a relationship requires both partners to show up and do the work**. By learning to work with our attachment styles and understanding how they impact our relationships, we can create deeper, more fulfilling connections with our partners.

Self-care (which we will be discussing in more depth in Chapter 37) is crucial when it comes to maintaining your emotional balance and navigating conflict. Incorporating self-care practices can help you stay grounded, making you less prone to getting activated and resulting in less conflict to navigate in the first place.

Remember, improving your communication skills isn't a one-and-done process. It's about ongoing growth and development. Be patient with yourself and others as you navigate this learning curve.

Lastly, don't forget the power of forgiveness. Forgiveness can help release tension and foster a more compassionate environment for dialogue and resolution. Forgiveness is about letting go of ongoing suffering, and it begins with forgiveness of self first (we will talk about this in Chapter 39).

Exercise for Moving Beyond Conflict: The Art of Repair

Resolving a conflict in the moment is crucial, but equally important is the process of repair after a disagreement. This process helps rebuild trust, deepen understanding, and strengthen your relationship. Here's how to effectively engage in conflict repair:

1. Regulate your nervous system: Before attempting to repair, ensure you're in a calm, regulated state. Use the self-regulation techniques discussed earlier (Chapter 32) to center yourself.

2. Take ownership of your part: Reflect on the conflict and identify your contribution to it. This isn't about assigning blame, but about recognizing how your actions or words may have impacted the situation.

3. Apologize effectively: If you've identified specific actions that require an apology, be clear and specific. For example, "I'm sorry for raising my voice when we were discussing our finances. That wasn't helpful or respectful." If you're unsure about what exactly upset your partner, approach the conversation with curiosity: "I can see that I've upset you, and I'd like to understand better. Can you help me understand what I did that was hurtful?"

4. Listen without interrupting: When your partner is sharing their perspective, practice active listening. Avoid being defensive or shifting the focus to yourself.

5. Offer reassurance: Especially for partners who fear abandonment, reassurance can go a long way. Validating their experience doesn't mean you agree with their perspective, but simply that you acknowledge it. Affirm your commitment to the relationship and your willingness to work through challenges together.

6. Plan for the future: Discuss how you might handle similar situations differently in the future. This may involve setting new boundaries, agreeing on communication strategies, or identifying triggers to be aware of.

7. Practice self-compassion: Finally, let yourself off the hook. Conflict is a normal part of relationships, and making mistakes doesn't make you a bad partner nor your relationship a failure. Practice self-forgiveness and use the experience as an opportunity for growth.

Remember, the goal of conflict repair isn't to determine who was right or wrong, but to understand each other better and strengthen your connection. By approaching repair with openness, compassion, and a willingness to grow, you can turn conflicts into opportunities for deeper intimacy and understanding in your relationship.

By approaching this work with curiosity, empathy, and a willingness to learn, you can strengthen your bond and deepen your connection with your partner. It's not about avoiding conflict, but rather about learning how to handle it in ways that expand your heart and enrich your connections.

CHAPTER THIRTY-FIVE

Trust & Boundaries

I HAVE NOTICED THAT those who struggle in relationships often have struggles with trusting others, and they also struggle to set appropriate boundaries. In this chapter we are going to talk about how these two things go hand in hand.

Trust is not built in a day. Trust is built *every day*, through the small things that show you are true to your word, and through the big things such as your partner having your back when it matters most. Trust is the foundation of any healthy relationship, and to maintain trust with another, we must build a foundation of trust within ourselves (we'll circle back to this in Chapter 38). To create lasting relationships, we must be truthful yet kind, plus be eager to make reparations when necessary. As we build the framework for trust, boundaries can be an exceptionally useful tool.

Boundaries are all about teaching someone how to best love you, setting your ground rules for how you will deal with conflict, and what you will and will not tolerate in a relationship with this person. Boundaries serve us inwardly by creating a distinction between where we end and others begin, and they are a proactive step towards honoring your true self and creating the meaningful relationships that you desire. It is crucial to note that boundaries aren't simply about stating your preferences—*they're your response to those preferences being disregarded.*

Boundaries are our way of telling others what we need, and our way of showing respect to and for ourselves. It's important to note that when you communicate your boundaries with others, "clear is kind" (thanks, Brené Brown, for this phrase), and that the timing of your delivery is important. It is best to choose a time where you are both calm, for example. There is no room for wishy-washy when it comes to your boundaries; set them clearly and uphold them fervently.

Still, boundaries within relationships can be a tricky topic to navigate, and it's not uncommon for people to struggle with enforcing their boundaries, especially when others don't respect them. Boundary setting is a skill, one that gets better the more you practice.

When it comes to boundaries, it's important to remember that everyone has different needs and expectations in relationships. Some people may have more rigid boundaries, while others may have more flexible boundaries. It's essential to understand your own boundaries and communicate them clearly to your partner or loved ones.

Reinforcing Boundaries

Even if you communicate your boundaries clearly, it's not uncommon for others to disregard them. When this happens, it's important to enforce your boundaries firmly but respectfully. This may mean having difficult conversations with your partner or loved ones and letting them know that their behavior is not acceptable.

It's also essential to remember that some people may be more likely to stomp all over your boundaries than others. For example, people with narcissistic tendencies or those who have a history of manipulating or controlling behavior may be more likely to disregard your boundaries. In these situations, it's crucial to be firm in your boundaries and to seek outside help or support if necessary.

One way to reinforce your boundaries is to have consequences for when they are not respected. For example, if your partner repeatedly crosses a boundary that you've set, you may need to consider ending the relationship or taking a break to re-evaluate your needs and expectations.

Boundaries are not about controlling another person; they are about taking responsibility for your own needs and emotions. By setting clear boundaries and communicating them effectively, you are creating a safe and healthy environment for yourself and your relationship to flourish.

Setting Healthy Boundaries

Start small by identifying your own needs and desires and communicate them assertively to your partner. Remember, *it is okay to say no and to prioritize your own well-being*. It's crucial to express your own needs and limitations honestly. If you don't have the resources to support your partner at a given time, it's perfectly acceptable to communicate that.

For example, you might say, "I understand you need support right now, and I want to be there for you. However, I'm going through my own challenges at the moment and don't have the emotional space to fully support you as I'd like. Can we discuss how we might navigate this together?" Remember, a healthy relationship should be able to withstand these moments of individual need and limitation.

It's essential to understand the difference between sharing our communication preferences and expecting another to meet our needs in a specific way. While it's important to express our desires, we must also remain open to our partner's unique expressions of love. If we're too rigid in our expectations, we may miss out on the beautiful ways our partner shows their affection. Remember, unmet expectations can limit our expression of love. Your partner may not always understand or agree with your boundaries, but it is important to stay firm and consistent.

While it's important to ask for support when you need it, it's equally crucial to consciously care for yourself. **Boundaries are not just about saying no to others, but also about saying yes to your own self-care.** This balance of self-reliance and interdependence creates a healthier dynamic in the relationship.

Finally, trust your instincts and listen to your gut. *If something doesn't feel right, it probably isn't.* Don't ignore red flags or dismiss your own feelings to please your partner or maintain the relationship. If someone is unable or unwilling to respect your boundaries, they don't deserve a seat in your inner circle.

In conclusion, trust and boundaries are essential components of a healthy and fulfilling relationship. Building trust starts with being truthful and kind, and maintaining trust requires a strong foundation of self-trust. Boundaries are a powerful tool for teaching someone how to best love you, setting ground rules for conflict resolution, and protecting your own well-being. By honestly expressing your needs, limitations, and personal challenges, you create an environment of mutual understanding and respect. By prioritizing your own needs and emotions, and communicating them assertively and consistently, you can create a safe and healthy environment for yourself and your relationship. Remember, you deserve to be loved and respected, and it is never too late to start setting and maintaining healthy boundaries. *The right relationship will not only survive these boundaries but will thrive because of them.*

Now that we understand how trust and boundaries create safety in relationships, let's explore how to actively solve challenges within that safe container.

CHAPTER THIRTY-SIX

Becoming a Solution Seeker

IN ALL RELATIONSHIPS, WE encounter challenges that put our connections to the test. It's natural to face ups and downs, but what sets thriving relationships apart is how we approach these hurdles. Instead of dwelling on problems, blaming others, or making excuses, we must become solution seekers—a mindset that empowers us to take radical responsibility and unlock the door to lasting change.

While it's important to acknowledge that relationships truly thrive when both partners adopt a solution-seeking mindset, this chapter focuses on what you can do individually since you can only control your own approach. However, I can tell you that when one partner consistently demonstrates solution-seeking behavior, it often naturally inspires the other to do the same.

Radical responsibility is about owning our thoughts, actions, and emotions without placing blame on others.

This means:

- Acknowledging that while we can't control others' actions, we can control our responses

- Taking ownership of our part in any relationship dynamic

- Choosing our perspective and the meaning we assign to situations

- Shifting from 'They need to change' to 'What can I do differently?'

For example, instead of thinking 'My partner never listens to me,' radical responsibility looks like: 'How can I communicate more effectively? Am I choosing the right time and approach? Am I truly listening to them?' This shift from blame to ownership is empowering because it puts you in the driver's seat of your relationship experience. When we take radical responsibility, we acknowledge that we have the power to shape our reality, not as victims of our circumstances, but as active creators of our destinies. Reject the victim mentality that robs you of your agency and potential. *Your happiness and fulfillment are not dependent on external circumstances, but on how you choose to respond to them.*

Becoming a solution seeker is a courageous journey. It involves embracing vulnerability, taking responsibility for our actions, and seeking growth even in the face of challenges. Every step you take towards becoming the partner you aspire to be is worth celebrating. Embrace the positive shifts in your mindset and the changes you bring to your relationship.

As solution seekers, we focus our energy on finding ways to address challenges instead of getting stuck in endless blame games. When faced with difficulties, ask yourself, "What can I do to improve this situation? How can I contribute to positive change?" By adopting this mindset, you become an active participant in creating the outcomes you desire.

This is where the *Flip the Script* exercise comes into play.

Exercise for Solution Seekers: Flip the Script

Just as I did the work to define exactly what I desired in a relationship, you too can shift from a problem-focused mindset to one that seeks solutions. By clearly envisioning what you want, you open the door to the fulfilling relationship you deserve. Here's how:

1. Identify the Challenge: Write down a specific problem you're facing in your relationship. Be as clear and detailed as possible.

2. Flip the Script: Now, instead of focusing on the problem, think about what you truly want instead. Write down your desired outcome. For example, if the problem is feeling unheard, your desired outcome might be feeling understood and valued.

3. Reverse Engineer the Solution: Reflect on what actions you can take to bridge the gap between the current situation and your desired outcome. List any practical steps you can take to create the change you want to see. For example, if you want to feel understood, consider having open conversations with your partner about your feelings and actively listening to their perspective. As you consider these actions, act with intention, consciously creating pathways toward your desired results.

4. Commit to Action: Choose one action step from your list and commit to taking it within the next week. As you take this action, remind yourself that you are intentionally creating the relationship you desire. Hold yourself accountable and check in with your partner about your progress.

By engaging in this exercise, you're not just identifying problems; you're actively creating potential solutions. Embrace this empowering process and watch how it transforms your perspective and your relationship.

Let's see how this solution-seeking mindset works in practice. Imagine your partner is consistently late coming home from work. A problem-focused approach might lead you to:

- Assume they don't value your time

- Feel resentful and hurt

- React with passive-aggressive comments

- Withdraw emotionally

In contrast, a solution seeker would:

1. Acknowledge their feelings without judgment: "I feel frustrated and unimportant when plans are unpredictable."

2. Consider various factors: Work pressures, commute issues, or communication barriers.

3. Have a curious conversation: "I've noticed you've been running late lately. Is everything okay at work?"

4. Collaborate on practical solutions: Perhaps adjusting dinner times, setting realistic expectations, or creating a system for communicating delays.

Holding a negativity bias—*in other words, expecting the worst in others*—can have a significant effect on relationships. This bias directly impacts our ability to seek solutions because it keeps us stuck in problem-focused thinking. This often means anticipating a negative reaction in advance, which can unnecessarily cause you to become defensive. What most typically results from this negative assumption—whether it was correct or not—is conflict and/or resentment. It is crucial to keep in mind that we humans do tend to fixate on the negative, but by being aware of this bias, we can discover different ways to approach our relationships that are less likely to contribute to conflict and unhealthy patterns.

Justifying our actions or behavior is a common defense mechanism that hinders growth and connection. As solution seekers, we must acknowledge our mistakes and limitations without justification. This vulnerability allows us to learn and grow, making space for more authentic and profound connections with our partners.

Open and honest communication is another crucial aspect of becoming a solution seeker. Instead of criticizing or blaming, practice active listening and empathy. Seek to understand your partner's perspective and concerns, and encourage them to do the same. Embrace collaboration as you work together to find solutions that honor both of your needs and desires.

Becoming a solution seeker requires commitment to lifelong learning and growth. Understand that challenges are opportunities for learning and personal development. Embrace the lessons that arise from your relationship experiences and use them to propel yourself forward on your path of self-discovery and connection.

In the realm of relationships, becoming a solution seeker is an ever-evolving process. It requires courage, compassion, and a willingness to lean into discomfort. But as you step into this empowering mindset, you'll find that the challenges you once feared become opportunities for growth, connection, and deepening intimacy. You're ready to dismantle the myths about love and relationship that have held you back, to step into your power, and to love and be loved with an openness and authenticity that transcends the ordinary.

So, take a deep breath, open your heart to possibility, and embark on the journey of becoming a solution seeker in your relationship. Every challenge presents two paths: we can focus on the problem and stay stuck, or we can redirect our energy into finding solutions. By choosing the latter, we not only improve our relationships but also grow into more empowered versions of ourselves. As you do, you'll find that the solutions you seek bring you closer to the love and fulfillment you deserve.

CHAPTER THIRTY-SEVEN

Self-Care Isn't Selfish

SELF-CARE IS NOT SELFISH, and it's time to stop believing that it is. *Caring for yourself well is actually the most selfless thing you can do.* Here's why: By building a foundation of unconditional self-love and acceptance within, you become stronger, healthier, and happier, and you increase your capacity to give to and care for others. In other words, **by taking care of yourself first, your capacity within your relationships will improve!**

Many of us have been taught that it's noble to put others first, and that self-sacrifice is a virtue. But this mentality can be harmful, as it can lead to neglecting our own needs and eventually burning out. *When you take the time to prioritize self-care, you set yourself up for long-term success, both personally and relationally.*

While the concept seems simple, many struggle to implement genuine self-care due to common obstacles:

- Guilt about prioritizing our own needs

- Fear of being judged as selfish or uncaring

- Feeling overwhelmed by others' needs and demands

- Limited time, energy, or resources

- Confusion about what constitutes true self-care

Understanding these barriers is the first step to overcoming them. Self-care isn't about escaping responsibility—it's about maintaining your well-being so you can show up fully in your life and relationships. I remember when I was juggling my own business, raising small kids, and trying to salvage my second marriage. I wore my busyness like a badge of honor, believing that neglecting my own needs was a sign of strength. I was exhausted, irritable, and felt disconnected from my partner. Instead of snapping in frustration, I would avoid confrontations and suppress my feelings, thinking I was keeping the peace. However, this only led to a growing distance between us.

To cope, I took up running as a way to escape the chaos of my life. I thought that hitting the pavement would help me avoid conflict and ease the mounting pressure I felt, but I soon realized something far more important. *I couldn't run from the one person I was most trying to escape: Myself.*

But then came a turnaround point. Running became a form of self-discovery rather than just an escape. It taught me valuable lessons about resilience and self-acceptance, and in an unexpected twist of fate, I even met my current partner while running a literal marathon. Prioritizing my well-being not only transformed my life, it also allowed me to build a loving relationship with someone who truly accepts me. *Talk about a photo finish!*

Understanding what actually constitutes genuine self-care is crucial. Self-care encompasses many dimensions of well-being:

- Physical: Exercise, nutrition, hydration, adequate sleep, regular health check-ups

- Emotional: Therapy, journaling, allowing yourself to feel and process emotions

- Mental: Learning new skills, engaging in creative pursuits, setting healthy boundaries

- Social: Nurturing friendships, joining supportive communities, asking for help

- Spiritual: Meditation, prayer, spending time in nature, connecting with your values

The key distinction between meeting your basic needs and true self-care lies in intention. For example, taking a shower because you need to get clean is basic hygiene, but creating a spa-like experience with calming music and aromatherapy transforms it into self-care. Similarly, eating because you're hungry meets a basic need, but mindfully preparing and enjoying a nourishing meal that makes you feel good becomes an act of self-care.

To identify genuine self-care activities, ask yourself:

- Does this activity replenish my energy or deplete it?

- Am I doing this from a place of self-love or obligation?

- Does this help me show up better in my life and relationships?

- Does this activity align with my values, well-being and intended outcomes?

- What would feel most loving or nurturing for me?

It's also important to recognize that while self-care is necessary, **we aren't meant to do life alone.** Connection and community are crucial to our well-being, and seeking support from others is not a sign of weakness. It's a sign of strength and courage to ask for help when you need it. By learning to ask for what you need and giving yourself permission to receive, you not only create opportunities for others to serve you (which can be a gift to them!), but your own needs end up better taken care of as well (win-win!).

Taking care of yourself doesn't mean that you must be selfish or neglect others, rather it's about finding balance and recognizing that you cannot pour from an empty cup. This journey is about finding the balance between caring for others and honoring your own boundaries, leading to healthier, more fulfilling relationships. **When you give yourself the radical self-love and acceptance that you crave, you begin to build an abundance of love and acceptance within yourself from which you are able to give.** Having this solid foundation will significantly impact all relationships in your life, without your having to wait for someone else to change.

Self-care requires both commitment and flexibility. Start small—even five minutes of intentional self-care can make a difference. Some days, self-care might look like a long workout and healthy meal prep; other days, it might be simply taking three deep breaths between meetings. The key is maintaining the intention of nurturing yourself, whatever form that takes.

A gentle reminder that the emphasis in self-care is on the SELF—*for those of you used to putting everyone else's needs first, self-care can indeed be a challenging endeavor.* I invite you to explore what truly feels loving and nurturing *for you* (i.e. catching up on laundry or taking care of your basic hygiene needs are *not* legitimate forms of true self-care, but requesting that your partner fold the laundry so that you can have a luxurious bubble bath could be!). Whatever self-care looks like for you, when you make it a priority you *will* see a shift in your experience!

CHAPTER THIRTY-EIGHT

Self-Trust

EMBARKING ON MY SECOND divorce taught me an invaluable lesson in self-trust: I learned that trusting in myself was about believing in my own ability to know what is best for me.

As you work to consciously create healthy loving relationships, one of the most powerful things you can do is to embody self-trust. The goal here is for you to recognize that you are a *whole person*, all on your own, regardless of your relationships with other people. This means respecting yourself enough to choose what *is* and *isn't* for you. **This means learning to trust your inner wisdom and taking aligned action from a place of confidence and trust within yourself.**

Self-trust goes beyond mere confidence. It's about:

- Believing in your ability to make decisions that serve your highest good

- Honoring your inner wisdom even when others disagree

- Trusting that you can handle whatever outcomes arise

- Maintaining your sense of self within relationships

Signs of strong self-trust in relationships include:

- Setting and maintaining healthy boundaries

- Speaking your truth even when it's uncomfortable

- Making decisions without needing constant validation

- Recognizing and honoring your own needs

- Leaving situations that don't serve you

Common barriers to self-trust:

- Past experiences of "getting it wrong"

- External pressures and others' opinions

- Fear of making mistakes or being judged

- Societal conditioning about putting others first

- Difficulty distinguishing between intuition and fear

- Previous betrayals of your own self-trust

Maybe you can relate to Cate, who had developed a poor sense of trust in herself due to past experiences of not following through. In her relationship with her ex, Cate struggled to follow through on the boundaries she set and, despite a bajillion promises to herself that if nothing changed she would leave, she worried endlessly about making the wrong decision. It's important to acknowledge that *not following through on the actions you'd like to take* is a common experience, especially when we are facing a great deal of uncertainty. Thankfully, no matter where you're starting from, every moment is an opportunity to make a new choice and build your self-trust. Just like Cate, who finally trusted herself enough to follow through with leaving her ex.

Building Self-Trust

Trusting your inner wisdom means listening to your intuition and paying attention to the signals your body is giving you. When you feel a strong sense of knowing about something, even if it doesn't make logical sense, *trust that feeling*. Your intuition is a powerful tool that can guide you towards your correct path.

Practical steps for strengthening self-trust include:

- Start with small promises to yourself and keep them

- Document your successes and inner knowing that proved accurate

- Practice sitting with uncertainty rather than rushing to decisions

- Build a relationship with your intuition through regular check-ins

- Notice when you're seeking excessive external validation

If you are having trouble hearing your intuition, one powerful tool you can use is meditation. Meditation can help you to quiet your mind enough to allow your inner voice to come through more clearly. Journaling is also a great way to connect with your inner knowing. Take some time to write out your thoughts and feelings and see if any insights or guidance comes through.

Additional self-trust practices to consider:

- Body scanning to recognize intuitive signals

- Regular self-reflection time

- Tracking decisions and their outcomes

- Celebrating when you honor your inner wisdom

- Learning from times when you didn't trust yourself

Trusting yourself is a process, and it takes time and effort, but it is worth it for the sense of empowerment and freedom it can bring to your life. Remember to be gentle with yourself and keep taking steps in the direction of your dreams.

Maintaining Self-Trust in Relationships

Once you have learned to trust your inner knowing, it's time to act. This means taking the steps necessary to move forward in your relationships, even if they feel scary or uncertain. When you take aligned action, you are aligning your actions with your true desires and intentions. This is the key to creating positive change in your relationships.

Key aspects of maintaining self-trust while navigating relationships:

- Setting and enforcing boundaries without guilt

- Communicating your needs clearly and directly

- Staying connected to your values when making decisions

- Recognizing when you're compromising your truth

- Taking space when needed to check in with yourself

Building confidence and trust within yourself is an ongoing process. It requires you to be kind and compassionate towards yourself, and to celebrate your successes along the way. It means respecting your whole self, including the parts you'd rather ignore, and *embracing your wholeness as if it were the answer to everything*.

Remember that self-trust grows stronger through:

- Consistent small actions that honor your truth

- Regular practice of self-reflection and adjustment

- Forgiveness when you temporarily lose your way

- Celebration of each step toward deeper self-trust

Every step you take towards embodying love and self-trust is a step towards creating the fulfilling relationships you desire. **You are the only one responsible for your own happiness *and* you are not responsible for (nor capable of) maintaining anyone else's happiness.** I guess what I'm really saying here is when you *stay in your lane* you'll experience a lot less friction in your relationships.

As you continue on this journey, remember to trust yourself, take aligned action, and celebrate your progress. You absolutely fucking deserve to have the love and connection you desire, and by embodying love and self-trust, you empower yourself to create the relationships you are worthy of.

CHAPTER THIRTY-NINE

The Healing Power of Forgiveness

As you work on improving your relationships, it's important to know that you have within you a magical ability to rewire your brain (creating new neural pathways with your thoughts) and improve your overall health and happiness (changing your body's physiological response). One piece of this involves releasing thoughts or emotions that are limiting you, and one practice in particular has the potential to completely change your life: *Radical forgiveness*.

Understanding True Forgiveness

What is forgiveness? The practice of forgiveness is designed to help cultivate compassion for both you and for others, increase your empathy, and help you to release negative energies that are keeping you stuck. Forgiveness is letting go of the painful baggage that you've been carrying because of something that you did not deserve. *Forgiveness is the key that unlocks the door to inner peace and freedom.*

It's equally important to understand what forgiveness is not:

- It's not forgetting or minimizing what happened

- It's not excusing harmful behavior

- It's not reconciliation (which requires both parties)

- It's not removing consequences

- It's not rushing the healing process

Forgiveness is a journey that begins with acknowledging the depth of our hurt rather than denying it. As we allow ourselves to feel and process our emotions, we can begin to make meaning of our experiences. This understanding creates space for us to consciously choose to release the burden of resentment or guilt we've been carrying. Through this release, we reclaim our power and free ourselves from the weight of the past.

Forgiveness is not about letting anyone "off the hook" nor is it about forgetting what happened to you. Letting go of stuck emotions that no longer serve you is for *your* benefit and therefore this practice does not require any apology or even acknowledgement from the other party. Ultimately, forgiveness is a gift that we can give to ourselves. It is a release from the burden of anger and resentment that holds us back from experiencing true happiness.

Whether you've been wronged or feel that you're responsible for hurting another, you've suffered plenty long enough. Punishing yourself repeatedly for your mistakes is a waste of time and energy, and you deserve to live a life free and clear of ongoing guilt or shame. While forgiveness is indeed a process that can take time, *radical forgiveness* offers a different path—one that has nothing to do with others and everything to do with healing yourself. You are the one with the power to release yourself from guilt, shame, pain, and suffering—no one else holds that key. After all, *what you give to yourself, you can then give to the world.*

Compassion for Others and Yourself

It can be beneficial to consider that *everyone is operating at their best, given the resources and understanding they have*. Remember the old adage "hurting people hurt people?" When you remember that those who have hurt you have also been hurt, it can help you to look at them and the situation with greater compassion, and this can in fact help to diminish your discomfort whether it be from fear, anger, frustration or other painful emotions.

> *"Compassion is not a relationship between the healer and the wounded. It's a relationship between equals. Only when we know our own darkness well can we be present with the darkness of others. Compassion becomes real when we recognize our shared humanity."*
> Pema Chodron

Unfortunately, we don't always receive this type of compassionate and loving response or support from those around us and if we are not careful, these fear-based behaviors may become all too common as we strive to create safety for ourselves. The good news is that you can create for yourself this very love and safety that you require and desire. It doesn't need to come from anything that is outside of yourself, in fact it already exists in abundance within you.

The Practice of Compassion in Forgiveness

Consider a time when you yourself have lashed out in pain and either intentionally or unintentionally hurt another. What you truly needed in that moment of pain was *love, acceptance and safety*. These are some of your most basic human needs, and when these are not met, it is easy to end up operating out of fear, attempting to protect ourselves.

When we're hurt or feeling unsafe, we often create walls rather than boundaries. The difference is crucial:

- Walls keep everything out, including potential healing

- Boundaries allow us to stay open while protecting our well-being

- Healthy boundaries actually support the forgiveness process

- We can be compassionate while maintaining our boundaries

"Shame is the most powerful, master emotion. It's the fear that we're not good enough."
Brené Brown

When you look at your own guilt and shame, it is also important to remember that *you were also doing the best you could with the resources and understanding you had at the time.* You deserve compassion, too.

What we need when we have made a mistake is not a lecture or an angry response, but rather compassion, understanding, and support so that we can learn from our mistakes and do things differently next time. **What we deserve in times of suffering is more love, not less** (thank you Matt Kahn for this powerful phrase). When someone tells you that you hurt them, you are better off believing them than to become defensive. Give them, and yourself, more love, not less.

The Path to Radical Forgiveness

Radical forgiveness has nothing to do with others and everything to do with healing yourself. It's about:

- Releasing yourself from the prison of resentment

- Choosing freedom over being right

- Taking back your power from past hurts

- Creating space for new possibilities in relationships

- Allowing yourself to move forward without waiting for apologies

Practicing Forgiveness While Maintaining Boundaries

It is crucial to create and uphold strong personal boundaries in order *to teach others how to treat you with love.* Good boundaries will serve to protect you from further mistreatment and unnecessary suffering.

This is especially important when:

- The hurt is ongoing

- You're still in contact with the person

- The situation hasn't been resolved

- You're working on forgiving yourself

Exercise in Self-Forgiveness: Oops! Let It Go

Ready to lighten your load? Let's embark on a mini adventure of self-forgiveness that's as easy as choosing what to binge-watch on Netflix. Grab a piece of paper and a pen (or your fancy journal), and let's dive in!

1. Breathe It Out: Take a deep breath, inhaling good vibes and love. Exhale any lingering oopsies.

2. Identify Your Oops: Write down a recent mistake you've been beating yourself up about. Got it? Great!

3. Own Your Humanity: Next to it, write "Oops!" in big, bold letters. Remember, nobody's perfect!

4. Plan Your Next Move: Jot down one small affirmation or doable action to learn from this oops or to make amends. Keep it simple—something like "I'm human, I'm learning," or "I'll reach out to apologize."

5. Celebrate: Whether you've written down one thing or a whole list, give yourself a mental high five! Then, do a little happy dance to celebrate your progress. Let loose and shake it off!

By acknowledging your oops with a light heart, you give yourself permission to be imperfect. That small step you wrote down? It's you taking charge and moving forward like the rockstar you are!

Remember that forgiveness is both a decision and a process. Some days you might need to forgive the same thing again and again, and that's okay—*this doesn't mean you're doing it wrong or that it's not working*. What matters is your commitment to your own healing and growth. As you practice forgiveness, you'll likely notice your energy becoming lighter, your capacity for genuine connection expanding, and your ability to maintain healthy boundaries improving.

The gift of forgiveness is that it frees up the energy you've been using to hold onto hurt, resentment, or guilt. This newfound energy can then be redirected into creating and nurturing the loving relationships you desire. With radical forgiveness, you can release negative emotions and cultivate compassion for yourself and others, ultimately improving your relationships and overall well-being. **Forgiveness isn't just about letting go of the past; it's about creating space for your future and the kind of relationships that truly fulfill you.**

CHAPTER FORTY

Relationship Green Flags

HELLOOOOO! #COUPLEGOALS

There's a lot of talk about relationship red flags these days, and I could give you a list of those from here till next Sunday. While being aware of potentially problematic behaviors and patterns is quite useful, focusing on what to avoid is only half the story. Here's why: **While knowing what to avoid is helpful, knowing what to *seek* gives you the power to create the relationship you truly desire.** It's an empowering perspective shift that can transform your approach to love and connection.

As I shared back in the intro, when I was in my previous marriage, my therapist encouraged me to create a list of what I thought an ideal relationship looked like, and if you recall, it was a challenge for me. I knew what I didn't want, but struggled immensely to figure out what I *did want*. When I started creating a list of my ideal relationship traits, I was actually *stuck*. My therapist had encouraged me to get clear about what I *did* want, but I was so used to focusing on what I didn't want, I could barely articulate anything positive. My mind kept pulling me back to all the wrongs I'd experienced, desperate to avoid experiencing them again. Slowly, she helped me connect to the desires I'd buried under doubt, uncertainty, and fear.

It took time, but we chipped away at those barriers until my vision of an ideal relationship—one that felt *true* to me—became clear.

Once I could see and believe in what I wanted, the way I experienced relationships shifted completely. This list of green flags became my guide for finding, and nurturing, a *perfect-for-me* relationship. In fact, I still have this list in the notes on my phone today. **Spoiler alert:** I used this list to manifest (i.e. find) my incredible partner, with whom I have brought to creation *every last experience and feeling* on that list.

And guess what? You can use these green flags as a guide for creating yours, too.

It's important to note that not one of the things on my list had to do with surface level desires such as physical characteristics or demographics. Rather the list was a compilation of the kinds of experiences I wanted to share and the feelings I most desired to bring into my reality.

So, let's dive into some "green flags" that indicate a healthy, thriving relationship—one that truly has the potential to stand the test of time. These positive signs may help you to create your own list or refine the one you've started. And who knows? This list might be the very thing that helps YOU to attract your perfect-for-you relationship, too.

Here are some key relationship "green flags" that you may want to consider for a happy, healthy partnership:

1. Complete mutual acceptance: You each embrace one another just as you are, without desire to change the other.

2. Clear understanding and secure connection: You both know where you stand in the relationship, fostering a sense of security and trust. When in doubt, you ask questions to get clarity, rather than making assumptions.

3. Comfortable expression and safety: You both feel free to speak up and express yourself without fear of judgment or rejection. You validate each other's feelings and this, coupled with emotional openness, creates a safe and nurturing space for their expression.

4. Making requests for your needs: You feel supported when asking for what you need from your partner and are likewise willing to support your partner to the best of your ability when they put forth requests. Neither of you is required to abandon your own needs to meet the needs of another.

5. Independence and interdependence: You support each other's individual goals while enjoying shared activities, balancing personal growth with shared goals. You encourage and support each other's self-improvement and self-care, emphasizing both physical and mental well-being.

6. Shared values and goals: You and your partner have similar values and life goals, creating a strong foundation for the relationship to be built upon.

7. Shared responsibility and partnership: You share responsibilities and contribute equally to decision-making, fostering a sense of partnership and equality. There is no scorekeeping and no competition. Love and support take precedence because you are on the same team!

8. Quality time and attention: You prioritize spending quality time together, showing genuine interest and attentiveness to each other.

9. Support for and celebration of achievements: You support and celebrate each other's achievements and aspirations, fostering a culture of encouragement and growth.

10. Sense of fun and adventure: You enjoy each other's company and can find joy and laughter together on a regular basis, even during challenging times. You approach life as the messy fucking beautiful adventure it is, appreciating the positive aspects of your relationship and learning from each other's experiences.

11. Intimacy, physical affection and trust: You express affection and intimacy in ways that are comfortable and satisfying for both partners and uphold a strong foundation of trust based on transparency in actions and decisions.

12. Healthy boundaries, individuality, and mutual respect: You respect each other's boundaries and maintain individual identities while still nurturing the relationship. You and your partner appreciate each other's uniqueness and create the space for individual needs and desires to be met, in conjunction with growing your relationship.

13. Active listening and effective communication: You both engage in attentive listening and ask clarifying questions with a genuine desire to truly understand one another.

14. Healthy conflict navigation: Rather than avoiding issues, you confront them honestly and openly, and work to resolve them together. You handle conflicts with respect and empathy, seeking solutions together. You constructively handle disagreements with win-win solutions and communicate respectfully even during conflicts.

15. Apologizing and making amends: Both of you are willing to apologize and resolve conflicts, prioritizing your connection over being "right." You recognize that it is far better to be happy and wrong than miserable and right. Your acceptance of one another, coupled with understanding the importance of forgiveness, allows you to continue moving forward without grudges.

16. Financial compatibility and future planning: You have open discussions about finances and joint planning for future goals, ensuring alignment in financial matters and long-term aspirations.

17. Mutual trust and reliability: You trust each other's words and actions, and can rely on one another during challenging times.

18. Appreciation and empathy: You each regularly express gratitude and appreciation, combined with empathy and understanding for each other's experiences.

19. Flexibility and adaptability: Both partners are open to change, and are willing to grow and evolve together when life circumstances shift.

20. Giving without expectation: You freely give within the relationship without holding expectations of something in return.

Of course, this list is not exhaustive, and you are likely to discover some additional relationship green flags—ones that actually signify a happy and healthy relationship that makes *you* truly fucking happy. Which is exactly what we're going to do next.

Exercise for Creating Successful Relationships: The Green Flag Adventure Hunt

To find additional clarity on what it is you most desire, I invite you to try out this fun and insightful exercise I call the Green Flag Adventure Hunt. Here's how you can do it:

1. Observe and note any green flags that you see in your daily interactions. Even if you're not currently in a relationship, you can observe relationships around you, such as those of family, friends, or even fictional characters.

2. Look for acts of kindness, effective communication, supportive gestures, or any positive relationship dynamics. These could be small gestures like making a cup of coffee for a partner or resolving a disagreement respectfully. Each time you notice a green flag, jot it down. You may also want to note the context and why you think it's a positive trait or action.

3. Reflect on your observations. Consider what these green flags mean to you and how they contribute to healthy and happy relationships. Notice how many of them you are currently experiencing and where you might begin taking some different action in order to create the ideal dynamics you desire.

BONUS: Share your stories or insights with others and celebrate the positive aspects of relationships together. Remember, the more we focus on the positive aspects of relationships we desire, the more we invite them into our lives. By incorporating green flags into your relationship, you can cultivate a healthy, positive, and fulfilling partnership built on trust, effective communication, and mutual respect.

I trust you're feeling empowered and inspired to embrace these green flags as you journey toward conscious relationships. By recognizing and incorporating these positive signs into your life, you're not just setting the stage for a thriving partnership—you're actively participating in the creation of your perfect-for-you relationship.

Throughout this part of the book, we've explored essential tools and practical action steps to help you navigate the complexities of intimacy, redefined what success means to you, reframed limiting beliefs, and looked at improving communication. We've also tackled the intricacies of conflict navigation and the transformative power of self-love. All of these elements are crucial in building the foundation for healthy, fulfilling connections.

Now it's time to pass the baton to you, dear reader. The next steps are yours to take.

In Part 4, we'll explore how to put these insights into action, so that you can truly embody the principles of conscious relationship building. This is your opportunity to align your actions with your intentions, making conscious choices that reflect the love and connection you desire.

It's time to step forward with courage, authenticity, and a commitment to creating the relationships of your dreams. Trust in your ability to manifest the love you deserve, and let's continue this adventure together as we unlock the next chapter of your relationship journey. It's time to answer the question: *What next?*

Part 4

Next Steps

"To love oneself is the beginning of a lifelong romance."
Oscar Wilde

CHAPTER FORTY-ONE

Create With Intention

THROUGHOUT THIS BOOK, WE'VE explored the complexities of being human and how we form relationships, diving into the perspectives, beliefs, mindsets, and patterns that shape the connections we cherish most. Now, in these final chapters, it's time to step fully into a new perspective—one of hope, empowerment, and intentional growth.

It's common to work on your relationship when faced with challenges, but true growth comes from doing the work even when everything seems fine. Don't wait for disaster or the lowest of lows to put in the effort. Nurture your relationship during the good times, celebrate each other's successes, and communicate openly even when it might feel unnecessary. By doing so, you build a strong foundation that can weather any storm and flourish even further.

This is where my CREATE method comes into play. It's a framework I've developed to help you intentionally create the life, love and legacy of your dreams. Let me break it down for you:

C - Calibrate Your Consciousness: As we've explored the power of beliefs, we've seen how they shape our reality and influence our relationships. But here's the beautiful truth—our beliefs are not fixed. We have the power to question them, challenge the assumptions we've accepted, and find our authentic selves in the process. We can calibrate them in a way that matches our personal vision for our life, love and legacy.

R - Refine Your Routine: Habits are the building blocks of our lives, and this is true within our relationships too. Just as a gentle stream carves its path into the landscape over time, the daily habits we cultivate can lead to profound changes in our journeys together. So, be intentional with the habits you foster within your life and relationship, choosing actions and behaviors that align with the values and aspirations you have in common with your partner. Seemingly insignificant steps taken each day can lead to extraordinary transformations over time.

E - Elevate Your Energy: Your energy matters and you can boost your energy through intentionally caring for your whole being. Just like a symphony's performance is improved through coming into harmony, harmonizing your mind-body-soul connection and operating from a place of unconditional love will help you to create improved life experiences. When you elevate your energy, you elevate your relationships.

A - Activate Your Aligned Life: You aren't meant to live anyone else's life; you are here to live *yours.* Getting aligned is about connecting with *your unique space of beingness.* It's about rediscovering and then confidently embodying *who you truly are* and knowing *what your purpose is.* When you're aligned with your authentic self, you create space for more authentic relationships.

T - Tune In To Your True Vision: It's time to start dreaming bigger and tapping into your true identity. It's about unlocking new possibilities as you envision the life, love and legacy that feels most expansive to your soul. Go ahead—be bold and unapologetic about your desires. Allow yourself to imagine your dream relationship, the one that fills your heart with joy and your life with fulfillment.

E - Empower Your Elevated Self: This final step is about truly embodying your next-level Self. It's about operating from a higher level of consciousness and becoming unfuckwithable so that nothing can stop your ability to create impact in your relationships—and in the world. This is where you take everything you've learned and *put it into practice,* becoming a living, breathing testament to the wisdom you've gained.

If you're still feeling stuck or are recovering from a relationship that has left you feeling pretty low, know that you are not alone. I hope you can feel the warmth of the energetic embrace that I am sending your way as I write these words.

I want you to know that the relationship of your dreams is possible, no matter how impossible it may seem from where you are currently standing. It may require some difficult decisions—releasing what no longer serves you, and getting clear on what you truly desire. It will probably also involve shifting your perspectives, questioning your responses, and understanding your emotions on a deeper level.

This journey of self-discovery and relationship-building is not about seeking perfection but about embracing growth. Each step you take, no matter how small, will bring you closer to the vibrant, connected, and fulfilling life you deserve. So, let's embark on this path of hope and empowerment together, ready to face whatever comes with courage and love. You have the power to CREATE the life and relationships you desire. It's all about intentional growth, conscious choices, and unwavering self-belief. You've got this!

Exercise for Conscious Creation: Future Visioning

As you embrace the various facets of the CREATE framework, know that you're stepping into the role of a conscious creator—someone who intentionally shapes their life and relationships with purpose and clarity. This exercise will help you envision and manifest the fulfilling connections you desire.

1. Set the Scene: Find a comfortable and quiet space where you can focus. Grab your journal or a blank page to capture your thoughts.

2. Ground Yourself: Close your eyes and take a few deep breaths. Inhale deeply, drawing in love and positivity. Exhale any lingering doubts or fears, allowing your mind to clear and open up to new possibilities.

3. Envision Your Future: Imagine your life five years from now. Visualize the relationships that bring you joy and fulfillment. What does your ideal partnership "look" and "feel" like? What values and qualities do you share with your partner? Picture, with as much detail as possible, how you communicate, support one another, and celebrate life together.

4. Write Your Vision: Once your vision is vivid in your mind, write it down, sparing no detail. Describe how you feel in this future, the experiences you are having, and what it is like to overcome challenges together with love and resilience.

5. Identify Your Intentions: From this vision, choose 3-5 key qualities you want to embody in your relationships. These might include qualities like being trustworthy, vulnerable, adventurous, or supportive. Write down your key intentions and use them to guide your actions moving forward.

6. Harness the CREATE Framework: As you navigate your day-to-day, use the CREATE method to consciously create your relationships:

- **Calibrate Your Consciousness:** Challenge any limiting beliefs that may hinder your ability to create the relationships you desire.

- **Refine Your Routine:** Establish daily habits that reflect your intentions and contribute to the quality of your relationships.

- **Elevate Your Energy:** Engage in practices that uplift your mind, body, and spirit, aligning you with the positive energy you want to attract.

- **Activate Your Aligned Life:** Live authentically, unapologetically embracing who you are and what you stand for.

- **Tune In To Your True Vision:** Regularly revisit your vision and intention, allowing them to guide your choices and inspire the actions that will make your biggest dreams come true.

- **Empower Your Elevated Self:** Approach life with confidence and resilience, knowing you have the power to create and nurture the relationships you desire.

7. Celebrate Your Role as a Creator: Take a moment to express gratitude for your vision and the journey you're embarking on. Acknowledge that you are a conscious creator, capable of shaping your reality through intention, choice, and self-awareness. By actively participating in your life and love, you empower yourself to design connections that align with your highest values and aspirations. Believe in your ability to create the fulfilling relationships—you will have them!

As you embrace your role as a conscious creator, you'll find that intentional creation naturally opens the door to deeper connection. When you're calibrated, refined, elevated, activated, tuned in, and empowered, you create the perfect conditions for true intimacy to flourish. This isn't just about surface-level changes—it's about creating the foundation for profound connection on all levels.

The CREATE method prepares you for the next exciting phase of your relationship journey: exploring deeper intimacy. When you're showing up as your authentic self and creating with intention, you naturally become more available for meaningful connection. Let's explore what that looks like...

CHAPTER FORTY-TWO

Exploring Deeper Intimacy

TRUE INTIMACY IS THE aim of doing this work. It isn't just about what happens between the sheets—it's a whole adventure of connecting so that you can deeply understand each other's hearts. It often involves a deep sense of trust, vulnerability, and understanding, where people share their innermost thoughts, feelings, and experiences.

No more holding back or tiptoeing around. Sure, it might feel scary, but trust me, it's worth it. Let's talk about the four types of intimacy:

Emotional Intimacy

Through emotional intimacy, you drop the masks and let your vulnerabilities show. Getting real and raw with each other, sharing your fears, dreams, and everything in between creates a safe space for each of you to be yourselves. With this type of intimacy, no judgment is allowed.

Intellectual Intimacy

Trusting each other so that you can engage in conversations that challenge your perspectives allows you to open up to new ideas, explore your passions, and take an interest in each other's world. This is where the sparks really start to fly!

Playful Intimacy

Laugh together, try new things, and embrace spontaneity. Being creative and playful is all about letting loose and having a blast. Who said relationships have to be serious all the time?

Sacred Sexuality

Get ready to rock each other's world in ways you never thought possible. It's not just about the physical touch, my friend—it's about being fully present and attuned to each other's desires. *Oh, and I'll tell you this: Eye contact can be a real game-changer!*

With this greater understanding of what intimacy truly is, you can make some real magic happen in your relationship. When you venture into this sacred realm, you'll feel a connection like never before. It's like your souls are doing a little tango, leaving you breathless and hungry for more. *Who doesn't want that?*

It's important to remember, however, that intimacy is a journey, not a destination. Embrace the adventure you've started through reading this book and watch as your relationship transforms into something extraordinary. It's time to break free from the ordinary and step into a world of deeper connection, growth, and fulfillment. **It's time to take your relationship from blah to bliss!**

So, grab your partner's hand and take the intimacy plunge together. It's time to create a love that defies limits and a connection that stands the test of time. Now is the time for you to create real intimacy and (re)ignite the fire within your relationship.

CHAPTER FORTY-THREE

Empowered Support & Accountability

IF YOU'RE EVER FEELING stuck and alone in your struggle to find the love and connection you're seeking, you don't have to go it alone. **Seeking support and encouragement is an empowered choice, not a last-resort obligation.** It can be a total game-changer when it comes to implementing new tools and creating healthy habits.

Consider enlisting the help of a mentor, therapist, or coach to work through your thought patterns and emotions as you uncover the shifts necessary to build the relationship you desire. *Even coaches and therapists have coaches and therapists because they understand the value of an unbiased and fresh perspective.* Regardless, be sure to choose someone who makes you feel safe and heard, without judgment.

When we're trying to make changes in our lives, our brains often default to old patterns and filter out anything that doesn't align with them—even new habits we're trying to create. This is especially true in relationships where conflict and struggle have been key habits; *an outside view can be invaluable.* It can help you see the possibilities and opportunities that are outside your current perception and keep you on track while you practice the art of consciously creating your ideal relationship.

Seeking support is a choice, not a sign of weakness. It's a powerful way to empower yourself and elevate your relationship to the next level. Accountability is equally important. Surround yourself with individuals who uplift you and hold you accountable for your growth. Share your intentions with them and invite them to check in on your progress. This creates a supportive network that will encourage you to stay committed to your goals, fostering a sense of shared responsibility in your journey.

If you feel called to explore this journey further or seek personalized guidance, I invite you to reach out. Together, we can work through your unique challenges and aspirations to help you create the love and connection you desire.

When you embrace support and accountability, you cultivate an environment where love and connection can truly flourish. **You're not just transforming your relationship with others; you're also deepening your relationship with yourself.** So lean into the process and let the power of support elevate your journey toward the love and connection you deserve.

CHAPTER FORTY-FOUR

Celebrate Your Love

CONGRATULATIONS! YOU'VE EMBARKED ON a journey of self-discovery, growth, and connection that has the power to transform not just your relationship, but your entire life.

In this final chapter of this book, I invite you to take a moment to celebrate the love you have been cultivating and the person you've become along the way.

Throughout this book, we've journeyed from understanding identity and mindsets, through getting unstuck from old patterns, into practical tools for transformation, and finally onto conscious creation. You've discovered that what seemed like relationship problems were actually opportunities for growth, starting with how you relate to yourself. You've learned to trust your intuition, honor your boundaries, and live with intention.

Remember where we started? With an identity problem that manifested as relationship struggles?

Look how far you've come!

You now understand that you're not broken—you're beautifully human. You've learned to embrace both/and thinking, to see triggers as teachers, and to practice radical forgiveness. Most importantly, you've discovered your power to consciously create the relationships you desire.

Remember, **the more you love yourself, the more you can receive and amplify love.** This journey of radical self-acceptance and authentic expression leads to a deeper experience of love and an improved quality of life in general.

Throughout these pages, we've explored the intricacies of relationships, shining a light on the beliefs, mindsets, and patterns that can either hinder or nurture the connections we cherish most. We've seen how your relationship with yourself sets the foundation for all other relationships, and how self-awareness is the key to unlocking growth and intimacy.

You've discovered that you can take control of how you see the world and what you experience, creating for yourself a new version of reality. *This power to completely change the world by starting with yourself is perhaps the most profound lesson of all as the miracle is always in the perspective shift.*

But remember, creating incredible relationships is not about seeking perfection or following a strict set of rules. This journey is about embracing the messy fucking beautiful, ever-changing human experience. It's about being present in each "now" moment, showing up authentically, and celebrating the unique connection you share with your partner and those you love.

Relationships are living, breathing entities that require nourishment and attention. Be intentional with the habits you foster within it, nurturing your connection with small acts of love and appreciation. **Embrace the ordinary moments, for they become extraordinary through your presence and love.**

As we near the end of this adventure together, I want to share one last powerful concept with you: *Turning your mess into your message.* We can't change our past, but we *can* change the stories we are telling about our past. That mess—your struggles, confusion, and pain—can now become your message. This is how we heal: *By transforming our pain into meaningful purpose.* I call it a "mess to message" because this process is about alchemizing our experiences into wisdom gold that we can share with others. Sure, the mess may still be there, but it's now also become a gift—one that can help others create their dream life, love, and legacy, too. Just as I shared my story with you, you now have the power to transform your experiences into wisdom that lights the way for others. Your journey from stuck to unstuck isn't just about you anymore—it's a gift you can share with everyone you meet.

You are absolutely worthy of love, joy, and fulfillment, just as you are. Embrace your imperfections and quirks, for they are part of what makes you beautifully human. **The relationship you have with yourself is the most important one you'll ever have, so be sure to treat yourself with kindness, compassion, and respect.**

As you look forward to the next phase of your journey, I want you to know this: *You have everything you need within you to create the relationship and life of your dreams.* You are the architect of your reality, the master of your emotions, and the creator of your love story.

Celebrate yourself, celebrate your loved ones, and celebrate your relationships. Embrace the messy, the magical, and everything in between. Love with your whole heart and show up for yourself and those you cherish with courage and vulnerability. Celebrate your love, celebrate your growth, and celebrate the magnificent, imperfect, and simply extraordinary human experience.

This is the end of our adventure together, but the truth is, it's only the beginning.

Your love story continues on and I can't wait to see the beautiful chapters you choose to write next. Cheers to you, to love, and to the infinite possibilities that lie ahead.

I love you! Now let's go do some epic shit, shall we?

♡ *Christy*

Appendix

More Inspiration and Information

Recognizing Abuse

Recognizing and addressing abuse patterns in relationships is crucial for our well-being and personal growth. Abuse can manifest in various forms, including emotional, verbal, psychological, or physical mistreatment. Recognizing the signs of abuse is the first step towards regaining control of your life and building healthier relationships. **It's important to remember that abuse is never your fault, and seeking help is a courageous act of self-empowerment.**

Radical responsibility is about acknowledging our thoughts, actions, and emotions without placing blame on others. When we take responsibility for our well-being, we become empowered to break free from abusive dynamics.

Breaking free from abuse requires courage and self-compassion. Recognize that you deserve to be treated with love, respect, and kindness. Seek support from trusted friends, family, or professionals who can offer guidance and assistance during this process. Remember that change may not happen overnight, but taking small steps towards healing is a significant achievement.

Reaching out for help is not a sign of weakness; it's an act of strength. If you're in an abusive relationship or have experienced abuse in the past, consider seeking support from a therapist, counselor, or support group. These resources can offer guidance, validation, and a safe space to heal.

If you need additional or more immediate support, the following programs provide resources, counseling, and assistance to those facing domestic violence and abuse:

USA:

- National Domestic Violence Hotline:

    - Hotline: 1-800-799-SAFE (7233)

    - Text: Text "START" to 88788

    - Website: www.thehotline.org

Canada:

- Sheltersafe.ca:

    - Website: www.sheltersafe.ca

    - This website provides a directory of local shelters and support services across Canada.

Please note that these hotlines and resources are available for anyone experiencing abuse, regardless of gender. They provide confidential support, resources, and information to individuals seeking help and safety in abusive situations. If you or someone you know is facing abuse, do not hesitate to reach out to these organizations for assistance.

Remember, in case of immediate danger, always call your local emergency number (911 in North America).

An Important Note About Your Mental Health

For mental health support:

In Canada:

- Wellness Together Canada: Call 1-866-585-0445 or text "WELLNESS" to 741741

- Crisis Services Canada: Call 1-833-456-4566 (24/7) or text 45645 (4 PM - 12 AM ET)

In the U.S.A.:

- National Suicide Prevention Lifeline: Call or text 988

- Crisis Text Line: Text "HELLO" to 741741

- Disaster Distress Helpline: Call or text 1-800-985-5990

For the most current information on mental health resources, please visit the official websites of these organizations or consult with a local healthcare provider.

Remember, seeking help is a sign of strength, not weakness. Your mental health matters, and there are compassionate professionals ready to support you on your journey to wellness.

A Message for the Mamas

Dear Mamas,

I want to share something deeply personal with you, something that I know many of you might relate to. For a long time, I found myself trapped in a place of indecision and uncertainty, unsure of what the right move was for my kids and me. I believed I was protecting them by staying put, fearing that any change might make things worse for all of us. The burden of potentially breaking up our family weighed heavily on my heart.

Yet, in the midst of it all, I couldn't ignore the nagging feeling that *something was off*. I had lost sight of who I truly was, my identity consumed by focusing on everyone else's needs. My voice went unheard, speaking my truth felt impossible, and somehow, I'd become responsible for managing everyone else's emotions while neglecting my own.

But then, a spark of curiosity ignited within me. I began to ask questions, not just about what was going wrong, but about what I truly wanted to create in our lives. An incredible journey of rediscovery and adventure unfolded before me, leading me to create my own happiness and find a love so passionate and fulfilling that I never knew was possible. I realized that to truly lead the way for my kids, I needed to walk my talk—to embody the qualities I wanted them to embrace.

As I reflected on what I wanted for my children, I came to a profound realization. *More than anything, I desired for them to become curious and critical thinkers, fearlessly expressing their authentic selves.* I wanted them to understand that they cannot truly feel seen, heard, loved, or accepted unless they show up as their genuine selves. I believe in their capacity to remain open-minded and kind-hearted, emotionally intelligent, and passionate about all they do. But most importantly, I wanted them to know that they are unconditionally loved and accepted, and that they have a safe and loving place to land, even when they make mistakes.

Then came a life-changing realization: I realized that I needed to take care of myself—to be the best version of me—to give my children my very best. It was a moment of power reclaimed, and it transformed not just my perspective but *our entire reality.*

So, my dear mama, if you find yourself feeling stuck or uncertain, I encourage you to consider this: *What if you focused on intentionally creating what you do want instead of dwelling on what you don't want?* **The power to change your reality lies within you, waiting to be unleashed.**

If you're seeking a supportive hand to guide you through this journey of empowerment and transformation, know that I am here for you. Reach out to me, and let's work together to turn your relationships from blah to bliss. You deserve to reclaim your power and create the happiness that both you and your children deserve.

With all my love,

♡ *Christy*

Love, Unstuck Bonuses

Ready to Take Your Journey Further? I've created some special (and totally free!) bonus resources to support your transformation. Simply scan the QR code below or visit loveunstuck.com to access:

Creating Love Sweary AF Meditation

Need a break from the traditional "om" and "namaste?" This unconventional meditation helps you align with the love you desire while keeping it absolutely fucking authentic. Perfect for when you're feeling stuck and need a breakthrough.

Self-Discovery Journal Prompts

Ready to dig deeper? These thought-provoking prompts go beyond surface-level questions to help you uncover patterns, explore values, and gain clarity about your relationships. Complete with space to write, this printable PDF guides you through the kind of self-discovery that creates lasting change.

10 Fun Ways to Connect with Intention

Because relationship growth doesn't have to feel like work! This playful guide offers creative ideas for meaningful connection that go beyond the usual "date night." From kitchen adventures to outdoor excursions, discover new ways to spark joy and deepen your bond together.

Visit loveunstuck.com to claim these bonus resources and continue your journey toward creating the love you deserve.

Create Your Happy Podcast

IF YOU'RE HUNGRY FOR more insights and inspiration on your journey to conscious relationships, I invite you to explore my podcast, "Create Your Happy." Available wherever you listen to or watch podcasts, this show is your companion in creating a life, love, and legacy that truly fulfills you.

From its inception, "Create Your Happy" has explored the most fundamental relationship of all—the one you have with yourself. Each episode offers fresh perspectives and practical strategies to shift your perception and improve every aspect of your life.

For those particularly interested in romantic relationships, Season 3 is truly a treasure trove of wisdom. It's dedicated entirely to the art (and science!) of creating conscious relationships, expanding on many of the concepts we've explored in this book as well as introducing new ideas to enrich your love life.

Whether you're looking to reinforce the insights you've gained from this book, seeking new tools to navigate your relationships, or simply want to continue your growth journey, "Create Your Happy" is your go-to resource. Each episode is designed to inspire, challenge, and support you as you create the love story you've always dreamed of.

So, if you're ready to take your relationship skills to the next level and continue your transformation beyond these pages, tune in to "Create Your Happy." Let's keep the conversation going and create some fucking epic relationships together!

www.createyourhappy.ca

Continue Your Journey with Personalized Support

Ready to take your growth to the next level? If you're feeling inspired to dive deeper into conscious creation and could benefit from personalized guidance, I'm here to support you on your journey.

I offer a range of programs designed to help you fully embrace your power as a conscious creator, particularly in the realm of relationships. Each program is built upon my signature *CREATE Method (below)*, providing you with a structured yet flexible approach to transformation.

Whether you're looking to:

- Gain clarity on your relationship goals

- Overcome patterns that have held you back in life or love

- Develop skills for creating and maintaining conscious relationships

- Alchemize your struggles, turning your mess into your legacy message

- Or simply accelerate your personal growth

There's an offering tailor-made for your needs and aspirations.

To explore how we might work together and find the perfect fit for your journey, visit www.coachchristyholt.com/workwithme. Here, you'll find details about my current offerings and how each can support your unique path to creating the life and love you desire.

Remember, investing in yourself is the first step towards creating the relationships and life you truly want. I'm excited to potentially be part of your transformative journey and help you unlock your full potential as the conscious creator of your happiness and love life.

The Create Method

<u>C.alibrate your Consciousness</u>: get curious about your beliefs and identity, and recalibrate them so that you can begin to create from the unlimited power of your conscious self.

<u>R.efine your Routine</u>: tweak your routine to create the most conducive environment for your success to be created.

E.levate your Energy: boost your energy through intentional work around healing and increasing your frequency to harmonize your mind-body-soul connection and operate from the energy of unconditional love.

A.ctivate your Aligned Life: connect with your unique space of beingness to rediscover and then confidently embody who you truly are and what your purpose is.

T.une in to your True Vision: discover how to align your actions to your higher self-identity and unlock new possibilities as you step into what feels most expansive to your soul.

E.mpower your Elevated Self: truly embody your next level self, operate from a higher level of consciousness and become unfuck-withable so that nothing can stop your ability to create impact in the world.

About the Author

Christy Holt, known as The Happiness Hussy, is an adventure guide, mentor, podcast host of "Create Your Happy," and international best-selling author. Her mission? To spread happiness around the planet by empowering others to CREATE healthy, loving relationships that make them truly happy.

Christy firmly believes we are all powerful creators of our own experience. Through her signature CREATE method, she guides whole-ass humans on an adventure of self-discovery and unlearning. As a mentor, Christy walks alongside her heart-led clients, supporting and loving them as they navigate their journey.

Her approach helps clients create a life they love, filled with authentic relationships and genuine happiness. Whether through her mentorship, podcast, or books, Christy's passion is clear: to help people recognize their power to shape their own happiness and create the deeply satisfying life, love and legacy they are oh-so-worthy of.

Pssst! Hey, gorgeous human!

One last tiny request… If Love, Unstuck has sparked something in you, created an 'aha' moment, or shifted how you see relationships, I'd be so grateful if you'd share your experience. Your honest rating and review not only lights me up but helps other souls discover if this book is their next step towards getting unstuck in love.

Please take a moment to leave a review wherever you purchased your copy, or send your thoughts directly to me at the e-mail address below. Your words matter, and I read every single one. Thank you so much for being part of this unstuck revolution!

E-mail: hello@coachchristyholt.com

Website: loveunstuck.com